Medieval and Renaissance Series
Number 7

MEDIEVAL

AND

RENAISSANCE STUDIES

Proceedings of the Southeastern Institute
of Medieval and Renaissance Studies
Summer 1975

Edited by Siegfried Wenzel

The University of North Carolina Press
Chapel Hill

March 9 78

Contents

Foreword

Once again, from 30 June to 8 August 1975, the Southeastern Institute of Medieval and Renaissance Studies, established in 1965 as a cooperative venture between Duke University and The University of North Carolina at Chapel Hill, opened its doors to forty-one scholars from all over the United States. It offered them the milieu, leisure, and library facilities needed to advance their post-doctoral researches and, through formal and informal contacts with fellow students in different areas of medieval and Renaissance studies, to deepen their commitment to humanistic scholarship.

The seventh session of the institute was held on the campus of The University of North Carolina at Chapel Hill. It formed the second summer institute made possible by a three-year grant from the National Endowment for the Humanities. Planning for the session began early in 1974 and was carried out cheerfully—despite worrisome delays and uncertainties—by a joint committee of faculty members from the two universities: Edward P. Mahoney, Dale B. J. Randall (co-chairman), Bruce W. Wardropper, George W. Williams, and Ronald Witt of Duke University; and John M. Headley, Richard W. Pfaff (substituting for Headley during fall 1974), Aldo Scaglione, Joseph C. Sloane, and Siegfried Wenzel (chairman). Besides deciding on matters of general policy, the committee was responsible for inviting the Senior Fellows, for selecting the Junior Fellows, and for giving its chairman and co-chairman much valued aid and counsel.

The session consisted of six seminars, each led by a Senior Fellow. The seminar topics and their participants are listed in the appendix. In addition to directing his seminar, each Senior Fellow gave a lecture that was open to institute members and the general public. These lectures form the substance of the present volume. They are presented here in a slightly revised form, with full documentation, though occasional touches reflecting their original form of oral delivery have been allowed to remain.

As director of the 1975 institute, as editor of these lectures, and as spokesman for all participants of this session, I take great pleasure in recording our gratitude to the National Endowment for the Humanities and to the two sponsoring universities that made the institute materially possible; to the members of the joint committee, who willingly gave their time and good judgment; to those officials of Duke University and the University of North Carolina at Chapel Hill who were directly involved in organizing and continuing the institute, particularly Provost Frederic N. Cleaveland of Duke, to whose sympathetic support of our aims the institute owes a very great deal; and to Professor Dale B. J. Randall, co-chairman for 1975, who has worked harder and more patiently than anyone else in our efforts to revive the Southeastern Institute. Special thanks are also due to Miss Madolene Stone, our secretary, and to the staff of the Humanities Reference Room in the Louis R. Wilson Library at Chapel Hill for their efficiency and willingly given assistance.

Siegfried Wenzel
University of Pennsylvania

MEDIEVAL
AND
RENAISSANCE STUDIES

I

Some Monte Cassino Scribes in the Eleventh Century

Francis L. Newton
Duke University

The revival of the venerable monastery of St. Benedict on its hill at Cassino was begun in the year 950 with the return of Abbot Aligern and a band of monks to the site ravaged by the Saracens almost seventy years before.[1] It culminated in a brilliant era—the second half of the eleventh century—when the prestige of the abbey was at its height and two of its abbots became popes. This rise from desolation and poverty to power and wealth included at least five kinds of activity within the abbey itself. The process of reclaiming and enlarging the congregation's possessions was one, begun under Aligern.[2] A very famous document of the year 960, which contains the oldest known sentence in the Italian language, records one of Aligern's efforts.[3] The acquisition and adornment of relics was a second. Many details of this kind of activity are noted in the *Chronicle* of Monte Cassino.[4] The elaboration and embellishment of liturgy was yet a third, especially the liturgy surrounding the three feasts of the Cassinese triad, St. Benedict, St. Maur, and St. Scholastica, falling as they did in the first three months of the year. In time this impressive body of lives of the saints, sermons, poems, and hymns was to include, added to the original nucleus of the life of St. Benedict written by Pope Gregory the Great, contributions by such diverse figures as Paul the Deacon, Abbot Bertharius, Odo of Cluny, Archbishop Lawrence of Amalfi, Peter Damian, and Alfanus of Salerno. An account of that process must await another occasion.[5] Fourth was the building of a church that would be a fitting setting for the relics and for the ritual so carefully composed. This task was accomplished in the dedication of the new Romanesque basilica on 1 October 1071.[6] The church was built under the leadership of the most powerful of the congregation's abbots, Desiderius, who reigned from 1058 to 1087 and who at his death was both abbot of Monte Cassino and pope under the name of Victor III. The fifth activity and the one that is in part the subject of this paper is the establishment and enlarging of a magnificent monastic library.

It is clear that the enriching of a library was felt at Monte Cassino to be part of an abbot's task. In this period of nearly a century and a half, from the reestablishment of the abbey in 950 to the death of Desiderius in 1087, five of the abbots left records in at least one book of their ordering that specific volume to be copied. Abbot Aligern himself (948–85) caused a colophon to be entered in a copy of part of the *Moralia* of Gregory, which he dedicated to St. Benedict.[7] His successor, Manso (985–96), in the year 991 left verses in a manuscript of Josephus to commemorate himself.[8] More verses were entered in a copy of St. Ambrose's commentary on Luke to celebrate the commissioning of that book by Abbot Atenulf (1011–22).[9] Atenulf's successor left his own portrait in another manuscript of part of Gregory's *Moralia*;[10] this was the famous Abbot Theobald (1022–35). And the most renowned of all, Desiderius, left no fewer than two portraits and two long subscriptions on his accomplishments, in lectionaries that survive today.[11] Incidentally, it is well that these abbots made use of the skill of poet, copyist, and painter to hand on a record of themselves in books, for most of the villages, fortresses, houses, churches, and lands that constituted the eleventh-century patrimony of St. Benedict have been lost to the monks, the Romanesque church destroyed even before the end of the Middle Ages, and the precious reliquaries and other liturgical furniture of silver, gold, silk, and gems stolen or otherwise dispersed and destroyed. Only the library survives, at least in some part.[12]

There are many ways of approaching a study of the medieval library of Monte Cassino and its contribution to the history of the West. Certainly the library can be studied and reconstructed partly by considering it in its historical setting of the other centers in southern Italy that used in a strikingly separatist and conservative way the traditional Beneventan script, at a time when most of the rest of Europe wrote the legible and comely Caroline hand.[13] One

may pursue the references to books and libraries in the *Chronicle* of
Monte Cassino and other historical sources for our knowledge of
the medieval abbey.[14] The literary works written at Monte Cassino
will yield important information on the authors, classical and patristic, who were known and read there.[15] But above all, it is
paleographical study that enables the student of this problem to
date and place the surviving monuments of the script. And of
prime importance among those monuments are the manuscripts
that are dated or placed by a scribal colophon, or whose scribe we
can identify.[16] This paper will examine a few of those scribes and
manuscripts on which scholars have recently discovered new information. In doing so, it will isolate and focus on a group of
activities that centered about the copying and use of manuscripts.

In an earlier study, I tried to establish a distinction between the
ordinary scribe and the scholar as scribe.[17] Of course, some Beneventan scribes whose names are known to us left a very brief
colophon. For example, Grimoaldus penned a beautiful lectionary
around 1035,[18] in which he is depicted kneeling before Christ, who
is flanked by the Virgin and St. Benedict. Beside the small kneeling
figure is written in red letters: "Grimoaldus diaconus et monachus
scrip[sit]." The miniature has great charm, but it does not give us
enough text to judge of Grimoaldus's education. Most of the colophons in Beneventan books are longer than this, and the scribes
have an opportunity to show their command of Latin, or lack of
command. When they write colophons of their own composition,
they often rely on traditional formulae, such as: "Tria digita scrib-
unt, sed totum corpus laborat."[19] As I have pointed out, "When,
however, they tried to add elements of their own invention, the
grammatical endings are faulty, the sense often becomes obscure,
and the metre limps or is completely abandoned."[20] An example
(not this time from Monte Cassino) is the subscription of the
Dalmatian deacon, Maio of Split, who wrote a lengthy colophon in
a commentary on the Psalms in Beneventan script, which is in
Zagreb today:[21]

Arbiter eterne. solus mirum qui fincxerat globum.; Iube hunc volumen tuo
sacro sereno aspicere vultu.. Quod pro suam.' Ádque suis debita.. Obtulit
domno paulus.... Venerabilis archiępiscopus hoc librum psalmorum. Ad
laudem sanctorum MARTYRUM.... Domnii.' Anastasi. Atque sanctorum Cos-

[5]

mas Et damiani.; Sed et vos quoque studiosi lectores.; Obnixe precamur. Ut cuique manu venerit. in vestris precibus Me comemoretis. Rex regum dicite cunti. Christe deus abde ei scelus.; Mê simul ínfimus Dīac Maioni scriptore. Ut et vos deum habeatis adiutorem.; Et in ęvum feliciter letetis.; AMEN.

Prof. Daniel Sheerin of the University of North Carolina and Prof. Leonard Boyle of the Pontifical Institute in Toronto have shown me how this rambling subscription was put together. In particular, Mr. Sheerin called my attention to the fact that Maio's third clause, "Iube hunc volumen tuo sacro sereno aspicere vultu," with its strange construction, is an amalgam of two expressions that Maio remembered from the Canon of the Mass. They are "Supra quae propitio ac sereno vultu respicere digneris," and, from the section that immediately follows, "iube haec perferri." The poorly educated scribe or one who was unpracticed in composition falls back on the colophons of earlier scribes or, in this case, on phrases from the liturgy. It is his failure to join these together in a correct form that betrays his inexperience.

In contrast, another scribe, and a very famous one, presents a colophon that is, with the exception of one little word, in quite correct and even elegant Latin. The scribe I refer to is Leo, whom Lowe called "the prince of Beneventan scribes."[22] His subscription is found in a handsome lectionary, which has always been at Monte Cassino. It is MS Monte Cassino (MC) 99, dated by the subscription in the year 1072.[23] Here a monk, who has been thought to be the scribe, is shown kneeling in a presentation scene that includes Abbot Desiderius and the giver of the book, the Archpriest John, before St. Benedict. Below, there is a four-line poem, and immediately following on page 2 is a long statement in prose, chiefly celebrating the accomplishments of Abbot Desiderius, followed by two further verses informing the reader that Leo was the scribe. The text is as follows:[24]

> Accipe dignanter quod fert pater alme'iohannes.
> Munus. et ęterni sibi confer munera regni.
> Supplicis ac votis pius inde faveto leonis.
> Est studio cuius opus actum codicis huius.;. .;.
>
> Anno dominice.
> incarnationis millęsi

mo septuagesimo secundo.'
indictione decima.'
Cum post transitum sanctissimi
et eximii patris Benedicti/
in hoc eius venerabili cęnobio
casinensi ubi sacratissimum
eiusdem patris et legislatoris nostri/
qui ipsius egregie sororis
Scolasticę corpora honorifice
humata quiescunt/ Septimo
et tricesimo loco domnus
Desiderius venerabilis abbas
pręesset.' inter cetera suorum
monimenta magnálium quibus
prę omnibus suis antecessoribus
mirifice floruit.' hunc quoque
pulcherrimum librum describi
pręcepit. Continentem scilicet
eas lectiones quę in vigiliis
precipuarum festivitatum.' id est
Nativitatis domini.' Sancti stephani.'
Sancti iohannis evangelistae.' Epyphanię.'
Resurrectionis. Ascensionis.' Ac
Pentecostes. debeant legi ~~~~~~~~~~~
Quem videlicet librum ego frater iohannes
marsicánę dudum ecclesie archipresbyter.
nunc autem ultimus eiusdem sancti loci famulus.'
ob meam meorumque salutem ex propriis
sumptibus componere feci. Ipsique sanctissimo
patri. B. eo die quo eius habitum suscepi.
super illius sacrum altare devotus obtuli.
Contestans de cetero. ut siquis hunc
quolibet obtentu ex hoc sancto loco
auferre presumpserit.' cum illis mansionem
sortiatur ęternam quibus in extremo iudicio
dicturus est christus. Ite'maledicti in ignem
ęternum.' qui paratus est diabolo et angelis eius ~~~~~~~~~
Quisquis tamen hęc legeris. Subiectum quoque
dysticon legere ne pigriteris
Huius scriptorem libri pie christe Leonem
In libro vite dignanter supplico scribe.;

Now all this—both sets of verses and the long prose dedication —is in flawless Latin. The author knows how to write idiomatic Latin with endings that are quite correct, spelling that cannot be faulted, punctuation that is sensitive and precise, and even accents here and there to guide the reader in the less familiar words. Furthermore, in the verses the scansion is correct and there is dissyllabic assonance in each verse, while the prose section manages long periodic sentences without mishap or loss of clarity. In the framework of eleventh-century poetic and prose style, the author, unlike Maio, is an expert.

All this technical literary skill might make one suppose that the superb scribe of MC 99 was also highly educated. Leo in that case appears to have been a master calligrapher as well as a fine stylist and scholar.[25]

There is a flaw in all this perfection, in fact, and it is the key to the problem. In the tenth line of the otherwise lucid prose statement, what the author should say is, "where of the same father, also our lawgiver, *and* of his glorious sister Scholastica the bodies rest honorably buried," instead of "where of the same father, also our lawgiver, *who* of his glorious sister Scholastica the bodies rest honorably buried." But the manuscript reads quite clearly *qui ipsius*. That is the reading in my notes, and Dom Faustino Avagliano, the learned Assistant Archivist at Monte Cassino, has recently checked the manuscript and most kindly assured me that it reads *qui*. A little thought shows that the error is the scribe's. He must have been copying a text that had an abbreviation he could easily confuse. What immediately suggests itself is the word *quam*. In medieval Latin, especially in documents, *quam* has wide currency in exactly the meaning we need here, in the sense of *and*.[26] We can surmise that the scribe had before him ꝙ the abbreviation for *quam*, which is not very common in Beneventan, and that he misread it for ꝗ,the universal Italian abbreviation for *qui*.[27] In other words, the scribe did not understand what he was copying, and that was because he had not written it himself. All this does not change the high position that Leo, "the prince of Beneventan scribes," occupies. The manuscript remains uniquely and breathtakingly beautiful. All it means is that Leo was not necessarily at the same time a fine scholar; and, in an age when Monte Cassino abbots became popes and Monte Cassino scholars became bishops and archbishops, we need not necessarily look for our magnificent calligrapher Leo—

who is otherwise unidentified—among the more exalted reaches of the Italian hierarchy.[28]

Let us turn now to three Cassinese monks who *were* scholars as well as scribes and whose identity is known, one of them from near the beginning of the eleventh century and the other two from its very end. One of the three is a well-known churchman and scholar. I refer to Leo Marsicanus, who, while at the abbey, near the close of the eleventh century wrote the admirable *Chronicle* of Monte Cassino and left to become Cardinal Bishop of Ostia at some time in the early twelfth century—between 1103 and 1109. A new edition of the *Chronicle*, to replace that of 1846 made by Wilhelm Wattenbach, is being prepared by Prof. Hartmut Hoffmann of Göttingen. Professor Hoffmann's keen paleographical eye has uncovered many details that allow us to see more clearly the activity of the abbey's scriptorium at the end of the eleventh century.[29]

The most fascinating manuscript of the *Chronicle* is one in Munich. Though written at Monte Cassino, it has lain in Germany since the twelfth century. It is MS 4623 in the Staatsbibliothek. Most scholars have agreed that its marginal and interlinear additions and corrections in Beneventan script have the flavor and appearance of the author's own changes. Only forty years ago, however, Klewitz argued that the changes were not the work of Leo Marsicanus but of Peter the Deacon, who continued Leo's *Chronicle* later in the twelfth century.[30] This argument was refuted decisively by Paul Meyvaert in a brilliant article in which he demonstrated that Peter the Deacon, though he received his education at Monte Cassino, could not write Beneventan script.[31] Building on Meyvaert's discoveries, now Hoffmann has shown that most of these corrections and additions are certainly in the very hand of the author, Leo Marsicanus.[32] More than that, he has discovered that a series of other manuscripts from Monte Cassino contain some writing in the hand of the chronicler.[33] A very instructive and particularly interesting example is the famous register of Pope John VIII. It has the distinction of being the oldest papal register in existence and fittingly has the shelf mark number 1 among the Vatican *Regesti*. Prof. Dietrich Lohrmann has written a thorough analysis of the creation of this very book.[34] The copy of the register was made by two scribes. In actual fact, a

third hand, an inferior craftsman, began the task but made such a
botch of it that he had to be replaced, as Lohrmann showed.[35] So
Lohrmann ended a long controversy over the strange appearance
of the first page. But after the dismissal of the hopeless bungler
and before the setting to work of the two copyists, a master hand
penned the remainder of the first column. What Hoffmann perceived was that this master hand is that of Leo Marsicanus, appearing here not in his role of author and reviser but in that of director
of the scriptorium;[36] or perhaps not director of the scriptorium but
director of the "team" that was deputed to make this copy of the
register. For, if Lohrmann is right, this manuscript, though created
by Monte Cassino scribes, was not created at the abbey. Lohrmann
will have it that the copying was done in the relatively peaceful
1070s, in the house of S. Maria in Pallara, a Cassinese dependency
on the slopes of the Palatine Hill near the arch of Titus in Rome.
Here the small group from Monte Cassino, directed by Leo, would
have had hospitable lodging in the city and convenient access to
the papal archives and to the exemplar of the Johannine register
that they were deputed to copy. If Lohrmann is correct, Cassinese
scribes were not content to ask for the loan of manuscripts from
which to make copies, but they themselves went, at least on this
occasion, to the source of texts.

It is interesting to observe, and certainly significant, that this
same papal register, which became part of the Monte Cassino library, was corrected by another famous scholar of the abbey—the
second eleventh-century scholar whose hand can be convincingly
identified. It is the hand of John of Gaeta. A younger contemporary
of Leo Marsicanus, John came to the abbey by the year 1068. A
prose stylist and author of saints' lives, he is credited with reintro-
ducing the rhythmical *cursus* to the papal chancery and himself
bore the keys of St. Peter, as Gelasius II, before his death.

Now what the eleventh-century hand wrote in the margin of
the register, beside a reference in the text to the city of Gaeta, was
the two Latin words: *Nota Caietam*. The same hand added the same
or a very similar note in three other places. Caspar long ago
suggested that this annotator who has such a keen interest in the
city named for Aeneas's nurse might in fact be the famous Cassinese monk whose home it was.[37] Lohrmann has now proved

that it is indeed John's handwriting.[38] What is of particular interest is to examine the types of corrections made by John in the register. We are gratified to note that he read the manuscript carefully enough to catch gaps in the text and to set beside them in his characteristic brown ink the letter *R* for *Require*.[39] But it seems that he did not then turn to the exemplar from which the manuscript had been copied to make good these lacks. There is no indication that he used any other manuscript of the register to correct this one. John's dominant interest, rather, is in the style of the letters, in choice of words, in spelling, and in punctuation. It is the stylist's instinct that is at work here, as befits one who was known in his age for precisely this care for the beauty, balance, and rhythm of his Latin.[40]

For my third example of a scholarly scribe at work, I turn to the first part of the eleventh century. It is a period of Cassinese cultural history about which we once were very ill informed. The *Chronicle* of Monte Cassino names no writers, poets, or scholars in relating the abbey's fortunes in this age, and modern histories are no help in filling the void. It was the late Walther Holtzmann of Bonn who first called attention to, and reconstructed the career of, an almost forgotten man who exemplifies the culture of southern Italy, especially of Monte Cassino, in the first half of the eleventh century.[41] That figure is Lawrence of Amalfi, who was a bilingual scholar and writer, monk of Monte Cassino under Abbot Theobald, archbishop of Amalfi, hagiographer while in exile in Florence, friend to Odilo of Cluny, and (in his last years in Rome) teacher of the young Hildebrand, the later Pope Gregory VII. Since Holtzmann's brilliant article, which reunited the scattered pieces of Lawrence's writing on the basis of a stylistic study, it has been my good fortune to uncover a really surprising amount of manuscript witness to the activity of this medieval churchman.[42]

Lawrence's Latin hand, for example, is seen in a manuscript of part of Augustine's *City of God*, which was copied at Monte Cassino in 1022–23. Lawrence was not one of the original scribes, but he corrected the manuscript, as he tells us in neat verses found at the top of the first page of the manuscript (MC 28) and later in the text.[43] Because of this autograph, we have a clear idea of the hand he wrote. We also have a clear idea of the kinds of corrections he made. Regrettably, he is no more interested in inserting the correct reading from the exemplar than was John of Gaeta. Again we find a stylist at work, one who was generally more concerned with correctness of spelling and punctuation than with correctness of the text.

Another trace of Lawrence's activity lies in a Latin manuscript that is today in Venice.[44] It is not an autograph. Yet it is so intimately related to the teaching of Lawrence of Amalfi (it even contains some of his writings) that its original must have been compiled by him. What it is is a handbook of the liberal arts; and since its script and contents show it was copied in Rome or the area of Rome around the year 1050, it may even be the very book that Lawrence used in his instruction of the young Hildebrand. The section containing logical works is probably the most significant; at least it seemed of prime importance to Professor Minio-Paluello.[45] The music section is also of interest. Included in the first or grammatical section, upon which I shall focus for a moment, is a long *florilegium* or collection of extracts drawing on some sixty classical and patristic authors. The classical poets are particularly well represented; they include Terence, Horace, Virgil, Tibullus, Ovid (many works), Persius, Lucan, Statius, and Juvenal. In the absence of other information about the classics read in southern Italy in the early eleventh century, this *florilegium* is of the greatest value. Because of it, we know what texts were available to a scholar who lived and worked in Amalfi and Monte Cassino in this age. The proof that Lawrence was the compiler of the *florilegium* lies in a series of manuscripts, evidence that will be presented at length at a later date.

A single final example will show how the modern reader, by examining the surviving manuscripts, may sometimes be enabled to see the way in which the monk as author used the library that was available to him. Again, it is Lawrence of Amalfi who illustrates my thesis. Among the books still at Monte Cassino that are dated by a scribal colophon is a book of saints' lives that one Martin of Monte Cassino completed in the year 1010 (MC 148). His subscription stands at the end of the original volume.[46] But another hand added one further saint's life—a Latin version of the life of Saint Gregory Thaumaturge, known, it seems, only from this manuscript.[47] I was surprised to realize recently that the Gregory life was written in a hand that has become very familiar to me—the hand of Lawrence. (See plate 1.)

It was said of St. Gregory that when he became bishop of Neo-Caesarea there were but seventeen Christians in his diocese, but that at his death there were only seventeen pagans. One of the wonders that was decisive in winning converts is recounted in the passage shown on the plate. The citizens of the town, gathered for a pagan festival, were lamenting the lack of space in their theater. They besought Jupiter in prayer for a remedy, with the lines here:

> "Iuppiter insignis, placide qui cuncta gubernas,
> Fac spatium largum ut possimus ludere laeti;
> Et tibi devoti persolvere carminis odas."

> "O noble Jupiter, who calmly rule over all things,
> Grant us wide space, that we may sport in joy,
> And with devotion perform our songs to you."

[MC 148, p. 519, col. 1]

The saint, hearing his fellow citizens' chant, sadly warned them that soon they would have more space than they even wanted: "they will be given space not for joy but sadness, by the bitter losses caused by death." The prophecy of Gregory is shortly fulfilled when the plague (the date is the early 250s) falls upon Neo-Caesarea. In their suffering, the citizens at last remember Gregory's words and turn to him, with a chanted entreaty that begins:

> Magnus amice dei; pastor amande nimis.
> Posce rogando deum; pellendo tristitiam mortis. . . .

> O mighty friend of God's, dearly beloved shepherd,
> Beseech, God, by driving away the bitterness of death. . . .

The plague can be checked only in households that do appeal to the holy man, and the curing of their bodies, as the saint's life has it, leads to faith and to the curing of their souls.

What is interesting about the copy of this life in Monte Cassino MC 148 is the copyist's additions. One notes the careful accent marks Lawrence has given, circumflex over long monosyllables such as *Ên* and *tû*, and acute marks over other accented syllables as

[13]

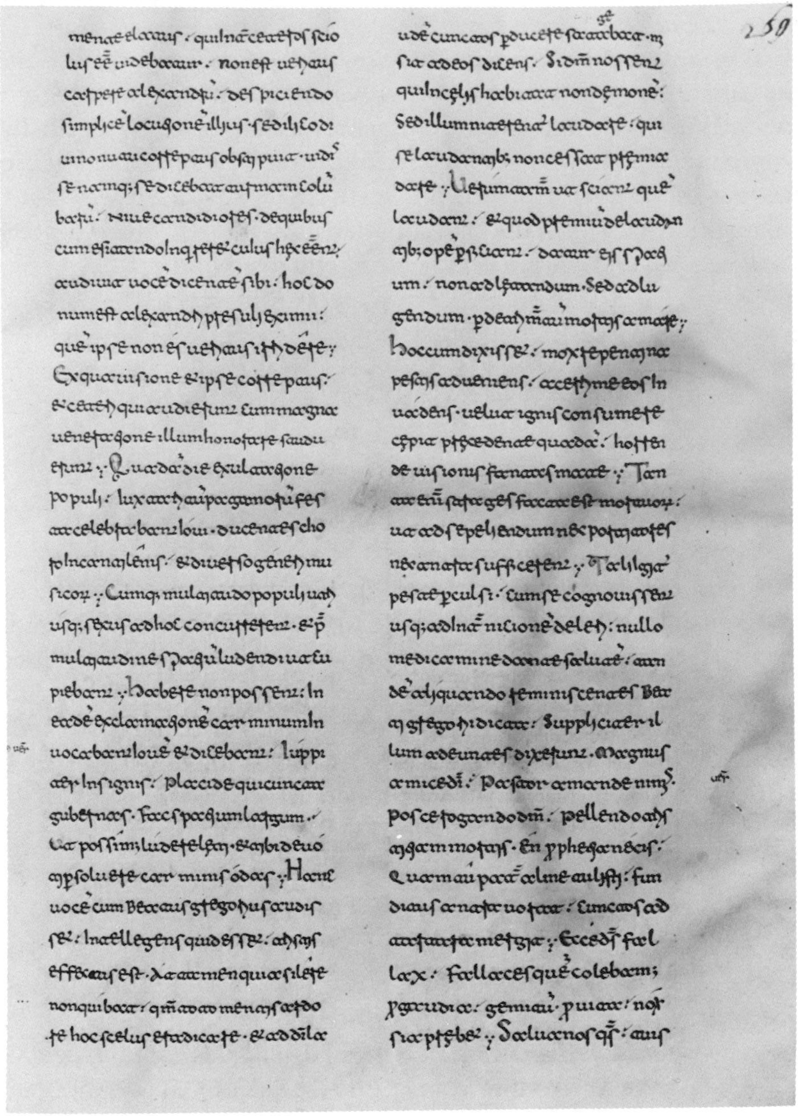

PLATE 1. MS Monte Cassino 148, p. 519, early eleventh century. Life of St. Gregory Thaumaturge.

in *nécis*. But what is more pertinent is Lawrence's way of recognizing that the entreaties to Jupiter and to the Blessed Gregory were in poetic form. The saint's life is written in what is known today as *Mischprosa*, in which there are numerous verses, two or three lines or more, inserted in the narrative, especially at dramatic moments.[48] Here, the appeals first to the pagan deity and then to the Christian bishop are couched in verse. The format that the copyist was using did not allow him to write these inserted verses *as* verse, but Lawrence shows the reader where they fall anyhow, by writing *ver* (for *versus*) in the margin beside them.

These marginalia become more significant when we observe that Lawrence himself composed the saints' lives that he wrote in the same mode—a species of *Mischprosa*. And in fact, this passage, from near the end of the *Life of St. Gregory*, probably inspired the form of a passage that stands near the end of Lawrence's *Life of St. Wenceslaus*.[49] To summarize briefly: A group of Bohemian prisoners, frustrated and grieving that they cannot join in the common celebration of the feast day of the martyred Duke Wenceslaus, address a prayer for release to God in a pure elegiac couplet:

> Who guiltless snatchest prisoners from the jaws of Hell,
> Look on us now for thy great martyr's sake!

Lawrence continues, "And when this prayer was done, as the fervor of faith sweetly warmed their inmost hearts, they began to raise their voices and beg for the intercessions of the aforementioned martyr, saying,

> Holy Wenceslaus, for us wretches help provide:
> Great martyr of God, be at your servant's side.

The martyred Wenceslaus's aid, thus invoked, is as powerful as the live Bishop Gregory's had been, and the prisoners' chains fall from them.

Lawrence tells the reader that this incident, which illustrates the great power of St. Wenceslaus, was related to him by one Dom Benedict, "a descendant of the tribe of the Saxons," who had come to live at Monte Cassino.[50] The story itself then is new (dating, it would seem, from the second half of the tenth century); the artistic form in which Lawrence cast it is derived from earlier models. The

Mischprosa form is well established in southern Italy in Lawrence's time, and I would not maintain that the passage from the life of St. Gregory Thaumaturge was the only model the author of the Wenceslaus life could have had in mind. Yet it is clear that Lawrence—perhaps he was reminded of the Gregory passage by the fact that both miracles are set on a feast day—took the story of Gregory as one of his models, and the discovery of Lawrence's handwriting and marginal notes in the Monte Cassino copy of that Gregory life shows us that he was aware of the artistic possibilities presented by a pair of verse entreaties set in the prose narrative.

This paper has focused, not upon a single large problem, but rather upon a variety of small details. It could not pretend to be a complete study of the Monte Cassino scriptorium, but perhaps these· different pieces of evidence, being brought together, have made the interconnected activities of copying, correcting, reading, and composing in one monastic house a little clearer.

NOTES

1. Dom Tommaso Leccisotti, *Montecassino* (Montecassino, 1971), pp. 53–55. The acts of Aligern are described by Leo Marsicanus in *Chronica Monasterii Casinensis* 2. 1–11, edited by Wilhelm Wattenbach, Monumenta Germaniae Historica, Scriptores 7 (Hannover, 1846; rep. Leipzig, 1925), pp. 628–36. This edition of the *Chronicle* will henceforth be cited as *Chronica*. A new edition of the *Chronicle* is being prepared by Prof. Hartmut Hoffmann of the University of Göttingen.

2. An exhaustive study of Monte Cassino's possessions in the Middle Ages will form a part of the forthcoming book by Prof. Herbert Bloch, *Monte Cassino in the Middle Ages*, to be published by Storia e Letteratura, Rome.

3. A recent facsimile is found in Dom Ambrogio Mancone, *I documenti cassinesi del secolo X con formule in volgare* (Rome, 1960), pl. 1.

4. A striking example is the gift of a relic, the arm of St. Maur, arranged by Odilo of Cluny after his visit to Monte Cassino in 1027; see *Chronica* 2. 54, pp. 662–64.

5. The most famous manuscript embodying this liturgy is the splendid Vaticanus Latinus 1202; for its contents see Bibliotheca Vaticana, *Codices Vaticani Latini*, rec. M.-H. Laurent (Vatican City, 1958), 2, 2:132–36, and the separate article by M.-H. Laurent, "Un antico lezionario cassinese: il Vat. Lat. 1202," *Benedictina* 4 (1950): 327–41.

6. *Chronica* 3. 26–32, pp. 716–23. The latest findings on the Desiderian basilica, as well as on the entire history of the successive churches built there, are now published by Dom Angelo Pantoni, *Le vicende della basilica di Montecassino attraverso la documentazione archeologica*, Miscellanea Cassinese 36 (Monte Cassino, n.d.). In an appendix to the same volume, Dom Tommaso Leccisotti gives photographic facsimiles and a transcription of the account of the dedication of the basilica, probably written by Leo Marsicanus, that is found in MS Monte Cassino (MC) 47.

7. MC 269, p. 13. For facsimile see E. A. Lowe, *Scriptura Beneventana* (Oxford, 1929), pl. 46. The text of this colophon and of the scribal subscriptions at the end of the book is given in a fresh transcription by F. Newton, in "Beneventan Scribes and Subscriptions with a List of Those Known at the Present Time," *The Bookmark* (Friends of the University of North Carolina Library) 43 (1973): 17–18.

8. The verses entered in a fourteenth-century copy of the lost Manso manuscript, Vaticanus Latinus 1987, were discovered by V. Ussani. See V. Ussani, "Un ignoto codice cassinese del così detto Egesippo e i suoi affini," *Casinensia*, 2 (Monte Cassino, 1929): 601–14. They have been edited in *MGH, Poet. Lat.*, V. 2 (1939): 412–13, no. 80. A new transcription is found in the present writer's article, "The Desiderian Scriptorium at Monte Cassino: the *Chronicle* and Some Surviving Manuscripts," *Dumbarton Oaks Papers* 30 (Cambridge, Mass., 1977). The present study is intended to complement the one on the Desiderian scriptorium. It deals with the crucial topic of individual scribes, which that paper did not attempt to cover.

9. The verses are in MC 5. For text see Newton, "Beneventan Scribes," pp. 21–23.

10. The miniature is on p. v of the manuscript, Monte Cassino 73. It is reproduced in Herbert Bloch, "Monte Cassino, Byzantium, and the West in the Earlier Middle Ages," *Dumbarton Oaks Papers*, 3 (Cambridge, Mass., 1946), pl. 218.

11. The first is MC 99, pp. 3 and 4. For a facsimile of the miniature and first set of verses, see Bloch, "Monte Cassino, Byzantium," pl. 220, and for the text of the subscription, Newton, "Beneventan Scribes," pp. 25–26. The second is the previously mentioned MS Vaticanus Latinus 1202. For a facsimile of its miniature, see Pantoni, *Le vicende*, frontispiece. The verses in this manuscript were published by E. Dümmler in "Lateinische Gedichte des neunten bis elften Jahrhunderts," *Neues Archiv* 10(1885): 356–57. For other facsimiles of the two presentation scenes, see Newton, "Desiderian Scriptorium," nn. 7 and 12.

[17]

12. For the history of the library, see the works cited in Newton, "Desiderian Scriptorium," n. 4.

13. The script is thoroughly described and analyzed in E. A. Loew [Lowe], *The Beneventan Script* (Oxford, 1914). The handlist of Beneventan manuscripts provided by Lowe in that book is further extended by his article, "A New List of Beneventan Manuscripts," *Studi e testi* 220 (1962): 211–44.

14. M. Inguanez brought together the scattered catalogs in his *Catalogi Codicum Casinensium Antiqui (Saec. VIII–XV)*, Miscellanea Cassinese 21 (Monte Cassino, 1941).

15. The study that most thoroughly traces intellectual life at Monte Cassino, at least to the beginning of the twelfth century, is that of Herbert Bloch, "Monte Cassino's Teachers and Library in the High Middle Ages," in *Settimane di studio del Centro italiano di studi sull' alto medioevo, XIX, La Scuola nell' Occidente latino dell' alto medioevo* (Spoleto, 1972), pp. 563–613.

16. A collection of colophons in Latin manuscripts appears in *Colophons de manuscrits occidentaux des origines au XVIe siècle*, Spicilegii Friburgensis Subsidia 2–3 (Fribourg, 1965, 1967).

17. Newton, "Beneventan Scribes," esp. pp. 8–11.

18. MC 109, p. 295. The text and a more thorough description are given ibid., pp. 16–17.

19. This phrase is found in many colophons from different parts of Europe and from different ages. In a south Italian manuscript, it is used by the Subdeacon Johannes of Monte Cassino; see ibid., p. 22.

20. Ibid., p. 11.

21. In Nacionalna i Sueučilisna Biblioteka, Metropolitanska 164. See ibid., p. 27. The punctuation of the manuscript is retained, whether it is point, double point, point and virgule, or two points and a comma. There are two erasures in the text, and each of these is indicated by four dots.

22. Lowe, *Beneventan Script*, p. 329.

23. For facsimiles, see above, n. 11. See also a brief discussion of the manuscript in Newton, "Desiderian Scriptorium." For a full description, see Lowe, *Scriptura Beneventana*, pls. 67 and 68.

24. The arrangement of the text in lines, the accents, the use of the hook below *e* for the *ae* ligature, and the punctuation are presented as in the manuscript. The pointing includes the virgule (/) for simplest pause, the point and virgule or point for a stronger pause, and the wavy line at the end of the long periodic sentences. The two sets of verses are closed by different versions of the Beneventan period, the comma surmounted by two dots (or, in the first case, three).

25. Such was the present writer's supposition in "Beneventan Scribes," p. 8.

26. A. Blaise, *Dictionnaire latin-français des auteurs chrétiens* (Turnhout, 1954), s.v. *quam*.

27. Lowe, *Beneventan Script*, p. 190. On the same page Lowe notes that there is no distinctive Beneventan abbreviation for *quam*. For this form of *quam* abbreviation in Latin manuscripts in general, see Lowe, ibid., p. 160; W. M. Lindsay, *Notae Latinae* (Cambridge, 1915), pp. 215–18; and D. Bains, *Supplement to Notae Latinae* (Cambridge, 1936), p. 35.

28. It has been suggested by Professor Bloch and Professor Klewitz that Leo the scribe was identical with Leo Marsicanus, the chronicler of Monte Cassino. See Bloch, "Monte Cassino, Byzantium," p. 210 and especially n. 152.

29. The fundamental article in which Professor Hoffmann has set forth his discoveries on the text of the *Chronicle* and its manuscripts is "Studien zur Chronik von Montecassino," *Deutsches Archiv* 29 (1973): 59–162.

30. H. W. Klewitz, "Petrus Diaconus und die Montecassineser Klosterchronik des Leo von Ostia," *Archiv für Urkundenforschung* 14 (1936): 414–53.

31. Paul Meyvaer, "The Autographs of Peter the Deacon," *Bulletin of the John Rylands Library* 38 (1955): 114–38.

32. Hoffmann, "Studien," pp. 113–38, especially pp. 125–36.

33. Ibid., pp. 127–36. The manuscripts in which the writing of Leo is definitely found are Munich 4623 (Chronicle of Monte Cassino), MC 442 (litanies and prayers), MC 280 (Guaiferius of Monte Cassino), MC 413 (Translations and Miracles of St. Mennas), and Reg. Vat. 1 (Register of Pope John VII). Other manuscripts in which Leo's hand may perhaps be seen are MC 234 (Life of St. Clement) and Vat. Borg. lat. 211 (calendar of Leo Marsicanus).

34. D. Lohrmann, *Das Register Johannes' VIII.*, Bibliothek des deutschen historischen Instituts in Rom 30 (Tübingen, 1968).

35. See ibid., pp. 9–27 (on the two scribes), and pp. 27–32 (on the scribe who bungled the opening and the master scribe who took his place).

36. Hoffmann, "Studien," p. 130 and n. 37.

37. E. Caspar, "Studien zum Register Johanns VIII," *Neues Archiv* 36 (1911): 89–90.

38. Lohrmann, *Das Register*, pp. 54–94.

39. Ibid., pp. 56–62 and pls. 6 and 10.

40. Ibid., pp. 67–94, especially pp. 76–80 and 93–94.

41. W. Holtzmann, "Laurentius von Amalfi, ein Lehrer Hildebrands," *Studi Gregoriani* 1 (1947): 207–37; reprinted in W. Holtzmann, *Beiträge zur Reichs- und Papstgeschichte des hohen Mittelalters*, Bonner historische Forschungen 8 (Bonn, 1957), pp. 9–33.

42. The works of Lawrence have been edited by the present writer as Laurentius Monachus Casinensis, Archiepiscopus Amalfitanus, *Opera*, Monumenta Germaniae Historica, Quellen zur Geistesgeschichte des Mittelalters 7 (Weimar, 1973). The study of Lawrence's literary activity will be presented in a monograph now being written.

43. Ibid., p. 43.

44. Venice Marc. Z.L. 497. A description of the manuscript and discussion of its connections with Lawrence are found in my article, "Tibullus in Two Grammatical Florilegia of the Middle Ages," *Transactions of the American Philological Association* 93 (1962): 253–86, especially pp. 274–80.

45. L. Minio-Paluello, "The Genuine Text of Boethius' Translation of Aristotle's Categories," *Mediaeval and Renaissance Studies* 1 (1941–43): 151–77.

46. The manuscript was described by Dom Mauro Inguanez in his *Codicum Casinensium Manuscriptorum Catalogus* (Monte Cassino, 1915) 1: 235–38. A facsimile is given by Lowe in *Scriptura Beneventana*, pl. 57. The colophon is given in Newton, "Beneventan Scribes," pp. 27–28.

47. Inguanez, *Codicum Casinensium*, does not mention that this text is by a different hand. The Gregory text is *Bibliotheca Hagiographica Latina*, Subsidia Hagiographica, 6 (Brussels, 1898–1901), no. 3678.

48. The mingling of verse and prose in the Middle Ages was discussed by E. Norden, *Die antike Kunstprosa* (Leipzig/Berlin, 1915), pp. 755–57. See also E. R. Curtius, *Europäische Literatur und lateinisches Mittelalter* (Bern, 1948), p. 160. The use of *Mischprosa* is well known in southern Italy, for example in Erchempert's *Chronicle*. See U. Westerbergh, Beneventan Ninth Century Poetry, Studia Latina Stockholmiensia 4 (Stockholm, 1957), p. 20.

49. See the edition of Lawrence's works cited above (n. 42), pp. 40–42.

50. Perhaps this Benedict came to Monte Cassino in the train of Bishop Adelbert of Prague, also mentioned in Lawrence's life of Saint Wenceslaus (edition cited in n. 42 above, p. 38). We know that Adelbert dwelt for a while at Monte Cassino in the time of Abbot Manso, probably around 990. See *Chronica* 2. 17, p. 640.

II

The Grail Kingdom and Parzival's First Visit: Intrigue, Minne, Despair[1]

Petrus W. Tax
The University of North Carolina at Chapel Hill

It has been said that the narrators of courtly romance try to make their fiction psychologically plausible.[2] This means, for instance, that the narrator justifies a certain behavior of his character or protagonist on the basis of the previous experience (or the lack of it) of this character. Wolfram uses this approach consistently and paradoxically with his Parzival figure—a technique that leads to the most catastrophic but also the most hilarious situations, since Parzival starts his knightly career *tabula rasa*, overreacts to new knowledge that he misunderstands, misapplies old experiences and teachings whose depth he doesn't fathom. But what is true of Parzival is also true of the many other figures that populate Wolfram's complex work. The reader must always ask: Why do they act or speak as they do, what do they know already, are they as well informed as the reader has been by the narrator, do they know more, less, or nothing at all? This leads me to a second point.

These dialectics of ignorance and knowledge on the part of the figures and of the reader are complicated still further by a specifically Wolframesque technique of presentation, that of withholding information at first, then providing it later or very late. The careful reader notices that he has to leaf back and forth, to readjust his own narrative experience, even to reinterpret it completely. This technique is at first maddening, then, as soon as one discovers that the narrator plays his game with the reader and tries to instruct and delight him, exhilarating and, I venture to say, redeeming. But it can happen that the careful reader has to forget everything he had gathered with so much trouble in order to evaluate an *Erzählsituation* correctly. Conversely, if a narrative context in *Parzival* remains too unclear, the reader might find the clue at almost any place in the work and will have to search. As a result, even the bold reader of Wolfram's *Parzival* becomes only slowly wise.

In another context I have suggested that any serious reader of *Parzival* should work his way through this story not only from the beginning but also from the end.[3] In close connection with the topic of my seminar, which deals with political, dynastic, sociohierarchical, and educational aspects of Arthurian literature, I would like to posit and to show that Wolfram intends, even forces, his reader to be highly politically minded. A reader who constantly has to check things told earlier or later, who has to reconsider and revise previous narrative experiences in order to see so many *gesta* of slowly wise kings and queens, princes and princesses in proper perspective—such a reader is not far removed from a modern politician and diplomat and, I submit, even less from his medieval counterpart. It will also become clear presently that Wolfram's *Parzival*, besides everything else, is a highly political work not only in its own subject matter but also in many situations as told by the narrator. One has to think only of the two great dynasties and the many little ones that intermingle and interact in Wolfram's work. I will say at this point merely that Parzival, within the Grail dynasty, is the only male heir to the throne who, having almost all odds against him, makes it anyway.

The narrator refuses to inform the reader, after Parzival's first visit to the Grail in book 5, about the state of affairs of the Grail dynasty and refers him to a later point, which appears to be Trevrizent's conversation with Parzival in book 9, on Good Friday. It is strange and a clear sign of nonpolitical approaches to *Parzival* that hardly anybody has looked thoroughly at the events of book 5 and their consequences in the light of the rich information provided in book 9. This is even more true for book 16, the last book of *Parzival*, in which the hero gets a second chance to ask the question and succeeds, where we have a second Grail procession, and where the narrator resolves everything unresolved in a most profound and most hilarious manner.

Let us return to the hero's beginnings. Young Parzival, bold but slowly wise from the start, crown prince of three kingdoms, is purposely raised by his widowed mother as a country boy, not as a prince. After his meeting with four knights, whom he takes for gods, he wants to become a knight himself; he leaves his mother, who dies shortly thereafter, not without having given him some good advice, which the youth constantly misapplies. He meets several people, one of them being his cousin Sigune, who tells him his true name, Parzival, which means *rehte mitten durch*, that is, "radical, but with a good or correct sense of direction." At Arthur's court he becomes a knight simply by killing the Red Knight, Ither, who is king of Cumberland, and by taking his knightly armor and equipment, all of which is red. Later, Gurnemanz teaches him knightly behavior in a very short time and gives him courtly advice, most importantly that he should not ask too many questions. By liberating the queen of Pelrapeire, Condwiramurs, from King Clamide, who wants to marry her, Parzival wins her as his wife (or rather she takes him). After more than a year of happily married life, Parzival asks for a leave in order to find out "wiez umbe mine muoter ste" (223:19). He will meet Condwiramurs again only after having asked the question and redeemed the Grail King as well as the whole Grail community, at the end of the poem.

He leaves by himself early in the morning. Riding the whole day without interruption, he reaches, at twilight, the Grail territory and sees a fisherman with others in a boat. His request for lodging is honored. Parzival's first visit to the Grail ensues.

Sitting in the great hall next to the Fisher King, suffering Amfortas, Parzival sees the lance covered with blood, the silver knives, the Grail procession, and finally the Grail itself, which provides an abundance of delicious food and exquisite drinks. But he doesn't ask any questions because his knightly teacher, Gurnemanz, had told him not to ask too much; instead, he says to himself, "I will find out from a squire tomorrow." Of course, the results of his failure are tragic, even catastrophic, but who is to be blamed?

If we follow young Parzival—he is still beardless—during the stages of his first visit to the Grail and during some time thereafter, we see events occurring and actions carried out that look strange and mysterious, and indeed suspect, especially in the light of the information given in later books of *Parzival*.

Let us look at Parzival's knowledge about the Grail first. It is very simple: *tabula rasa*. Parzival, when arriving, doesn't know anything about the Grail, the dynasty, the castle, or the community. The Grail community, on the other hand, the Grail King included, appears not to be aware of the fact that Parzival, Herzeloyde's son and therefore a possible heir to the Grail, exists. To give the reasons for this ignorance of the Grail people would require another paper.

But for the Grail community, especially for the Grail King and his inner circle, this visit is connected with strict stipulations. Much later, in the Good Friday episode, Trevrizent tells Parzival that after it became manifest that Amfortas's wound couldn't be cured with normal medicine, the Grail community started praying to God:

> unser venje viel wir für den gral.
> dar an gesah wir zeinem mal
> geschriben, dar solde ein riter komn:
> wurd des frage alda vernomn,
> so solde der kumber ende han:
> ez waere kint magt ode man,
> daz in der frage warnet iht,
> sone solt diu frage helfen niht,
> wan daz der schade stüende als e
> und herzelicher taete we.
> diu schrift sprach: "habt ir daz vernomn?
> iwer warnen mac ze schaden komn.
> Fragt er niht bi der ersten naht,
> so zerget siner frage maht.
> wirt sin frage an rehter zit getan,
> so sol erz künecriche han,
> unt hat der kumber ende
> von der hohsten hende.
> da mit ist Anfortas genesen,
> ern sol aber niemer künec wesen."
>
> [483:19–484:8]

We fell on our knees in prayer before the Grail. All at once we saw written upon it that a knight should come, and if from him a question came, our

[23]

sorrow would be ended, but if anyone, child or maid or man, should prompt him in any way to the question, his question would not help, but the wound would remain as before and pain more violently. The writing said, "Have you understood? Any prompting from you can do harm. If he does not ask the first night, the power of his question will vanish. But if at the right time his question is asked, he shall be king of the realm and an end shall be made of your sorrow by the hand of the Highest. Then Amfortas shall be healed, but he shall no longer be king." [Mustard/Passage, pp. 258f.]

This passage appears to make three points very clear: the divine authority behind the Grail insists that the question may be asked during the first night only;[4] any prompting would be dangerous; Amfortas would cease to be king and the man who asked the question would succeed him. It is important to keep in mind that Parzival, at the time of his first visit, didn't know anything about this; the Grail community, however, was very well informed about these conditions.

Let us look now at those mysterious and suspect events that I mentioned before.

First, why was youthful Parzival admitted at all and later on subjected to the Grail procession and its consequences?

Second, after squires have led Parzival's horse away and taken off his armor, and Parzival has washed himself, the narrator says:

> gar von allem tadel vri
> mit pfelle von Arabi
> man truoc im einen mantel dar:
> den legt an sich der wol gevar;
>
> [228:7–10]

They brought him a cloak of flawless Arabian silk, and the fair youth put it on. [Mustard/Passage, p. 125]

This looks to me very much like royal investiture, or at least an anticipation of it, the royal mantle being one of the *Herrschaftszeichen* in Schramm's terminology.[5] If so, it would be a clear case of prompting, not with words, but with gestures.

In addition, shortly thereafter the narrator inserts a little scene:

Sin harnasch was von im getragen:
daz begunder sider klagen,
da er sich schimpfes niht versan.
ze hove ein redespaeher man
bat komn ze vrävelliche
den gast ellens riche
zem wirte, als ob im waere zorn.
des het er nach den lip verlorn
von dem jungen Parzival.
do er sin swert wol gemal
ninder bi im ligen vant,
zer fiuste twanger sus die hant
daz dez pluot uzen nagelen schoz
und im den ermel gar begoz.
"nein, herre," sprach diu ritterschaft,
"ez ist ein man der schimpfes kraft
hat, swie trurc wir anders sin:
tuot iwer zuht gein im schin."

[229:1–18]

His armor was removed and taken away. This he regretted a moment later when he was made the butt of a joke which he did not understand. A man of the court, known for his ambiguous speech, now invited his valiant guest to join his host, but in an all too arrogant tone, as though he were angry. For that he came near to losing his life at the hands of the young Parzival, who, finding his bright sword nowhere at hand, clenched his fist so tightly that the blood gushed out from beneath his nails and wet the sleeve of his cloak. "O Sir, not so," said the knights, "he is a man who likes to joke, however sad we are otherwise. Show yourself courteous toward him." [Mustard/Passage, p. 125f.]

This is a psychological masterpiece. It shows dramatically how awkwardly and immaturely Parzival reacts; instead of asking something like, "What do you mean, Sir?"—asking a sensible question, possibly *the* question!—he is so tense that he can think only of brute force. How can a young man, so prone to ire and instant revenge, even under stress, be ready for the kingship of the highest empire in Wolfram's fictional world? On the other hand, why would this courtier want to push the guest into the great hall?

Fourth, the Grail procession consists of twenty-five maidens, not little girls in white, as one might expect, but ladies of the highest nobility, all dressed in the most lavish and colorful garments, the twenty-fifth being Queen Repanse de Joie, Amfortas's sister, who carries the Grail. The narrator describes all of them in minute detail, using in a subdued way several tricks to indicate the distinct erotic character of the procession: some wear flowery wreaths as in spring, others have red, fiery lips, their narrow waistlines are stressed; the most radiant is Queen Repanse.[6] Let us suppose for a moment that this eroticism leads up to Repanse and that the visitor were to fall in love with her. We then would have had the weird situation that young Parzival would or could have fallen in love with his own aunt. Is the Grail community expecting somebody else?

Furthermore, toward the end of the meal and after Parzival had decided not to ask any questions at this time, Amfortas gives Parzival a most precious sword. Again, politically speaking, this looks very much like entrusting the sword to the new king and the transfer of royal power—another *Herrschaftszeichen*. And another case of prompting as well.

Finally, a few days later Parzival returns to Arthur's court. He is now officially introduced as a new member of the Round Table. But exactly at this high point of his knightly career, the extremely ugly female messenger of the Grail castle, Cundrie, appears, and curses and condemns young Parzival in the presence of the whole Arthurian court. Every gesture and every word of hers betray her despair, but the reader is almost horrified by the fierceness of her verbal attack on Parzival, which comes very close to character assassination. Since the reader knows about Parzival's naivete, Cundrie's words boomerang at once. If, in addition, she is the spokeswoman for the Grail community and especially for King Amfortas and his inner circle, her self-righteousness is indicative of an attitude that is far removed from any ideal of kingship and royal prudence. Is the Grail dynasty, particularly King Amfortas, already (or again) worthy to be redeemed?

Let us try to shed some light on the issues raised above. It is clear that Amfortas is an impotent king in almost every respect.

The Grail message indicated that he would abdicate as soon as the question had been asked. For him, a successor from within the Grail dynasty is not in sight. The reader knows that Parzival is the only possible candidate, but there is no evidence that Amfortas and the Grail community are aware of Parzival's existence at the time of his first visit. For Amfortas only two possibilities exist: the expected visitor, while belonging to another dynasty, is either married or unmarried. If he is married, the Grail dynasty would be replaced by the dynasty of the visitor. That this would be an extremely painful change for the proud Grail family, the first Christian dynasty to which God had entrusted the care of the Holy Grail, is evident. If unmarried, however, the visitor could be brought into the Grail dynasty—by means of a marriage. Queen Repanse, Amfortas's only surviving sister, is for him the highest political trump card because the continuation of the Grail dynasty is dependent upon her and her progeny.

We are ready now for an important question: Who is the visitor coming to the Grail that night? If you say, "Parzival, of course!" you are right—and wrong. You are right as an objective reader, wrong as a subjective reader who would look at the guest with Amfortas's eyes. Who comes to Amfortas? The Red Knight! The narrator tells us that although it is twilight, Parzival sees the hat made out of peacock feathers that the Fisher King wears (225:8–12). It seems impossible that Amfortas would not have seen the arriving stranger's red armor.

In addition, Amfortas certainly was acquainted with the Red Knight, for we hear—again much later—from Trevrizent in book 9 that the Red Knight had been his, Trevrizent's, squire twenty to twenty-five years ago, given to him by Gahmuret, Parzival's father, shortly before he was killed (498:13–16). Amfortas must have known, too, that the Red Knight was King Arthur's only cousin and, at that time, the crown prince of Cumberland (he is king of Cumberland when killed by Parzival, but apparently Amfortas had not been informed about this killing). Whether the Red Knight ever married remains uncertain. But that Ither was a favorite with the other sex must have been already evident to Amfortas when he was still Trevrizent's squire.

Let us look again at Amfortas himself and his situation at the time of Parzival's first visit. As you remember, the Grail King had been wounded in his testicles when he was a young man. For about twenty to twenty-five years he had suffered intense pains. Again much later we hear that his pains this evening were extreme because of the position of the stars, especially of Saturn (cf. 489: 22–29). After the message on the Grail about a possible savior appeared, he must have concluded that finally perhaps the right time has come. The Red Knight at this point was his only chance, politically and humanly, and he might have appeared to Amfortas as a rather suitable successor, even if he belonged to Arthur's dynasty. The Fisher King, therefore, admits him readily. But the Red Knight not only had to ask the question; for dynastic reasons he had to fall in love with Queen Repanse as well (or perhaps, he had to fall in love with Repanse first and ask the question then—out of love).

If the rituals during this visit were aimed at the Red Knight as a *minnaere* and royal husband for Queen Repanse, several events that I mentioned before fall into place: the mantle the visitor received *was* a sign of investiture, the sword *was* a symbol of transfer of royal power, the eroticization of the Grail procession *was* intended to match the Red Knight with Queen Repanse.

But at this point *zwivel* befell me. Was it conceivable that the Grail King Amfortas was the mastermind behind such a political scheme? Would he interpret the command of the Grail not to prompt in such a narrow way as to believe that prompting by more or less symbolic gestures would not be considered as real prompting by the divine authority behind the Grail? Would he ruthlessly dare to eroticize the procession of the Holy Grail specifically for dynastic purposes, thus trying to take fate, fortune, and future into his own hands? More evidence seemed to be necessary.

Checking back, I found three things:

1. The mantle the visitor received at the beginning is made of *pfelle von Arabi*. The dress Queen Repanse wears during the Grail procession is made of the same precious material (235:18 f.), whereas the garments of the twenty-four other ladies are all made of other stuff.

2. The erotic features of the ladies in the Grail procession follow a general pattern that moves downward—running counter to the

ranks of the ladies, namely from a generally love-arousing appearance and flowery wreaths on the heads (232:11–17) via red, burn-
ing lips and narrow waistlines to *geteilte röcke* (cf. 235:13), skirts
with a slit or slits. I must stress, though, that the queen, Repanse,
altogether lacks such features; she is all radiance.

3. Soon after the meal the visitor is led to his sleeping quarters.
The narrator says:

> der wirt bot im guote naht.
> diu riterschaft do gar uf spranc.
> ein teil ir im dar naher dranc:
> do fuorten si den jungen man
> in eine kemenaten san.
> diu was also geheret
> mit einem bette geret,
> daz mich min armuot immer müet,
> sit d'erde alsölhe richheit blüet.
> Dem bette armuot was tiur.
> alser glohte in eime fiur,
> lac druffe ein pfellel lieht gemal.
> die ritter bat do Parzival
> wider varen an ir gemach,
> do'r da niht mer bette sach.
>
> [242:22–243:6]

His host bade him good night. The knights all sprang up from their seats,
and a group of them came to lead the young man to his room. It was richly
decorated, with a bed so sumptuous that I am irked at my own poverty in
a world which contains such riches. There was no poverty about that bed.
A bright pfellel-silk covered it, the colors glowing as if on fire. Parzival,
seeing that there were no beds save the one, bade the knights go to their
rest. [Mustard/Passage, p. 132]

I submit that we are here in the royal bedchamber of the Grail
castle, a room that had not been used properly at least since Amfortas's wounding, that the fiery red cover matches the Red Knight's
redness perfectly and purposely, and that we are confronted here
with a real king-size bed, intended for King Ither and Queen Repanse.

But I was not altogether satisfied. Upon reflection it came to

mind again that there is a second Grail procession in Wolfram's
Parzival, at the very end of the work. Here in book 16 it finally
happens that Parzival, accompanied by his black-and-white half
brother, speckled Feirefiz, asks the question. Amfortas is healed
and restored to his former beauty, the Grail family is united, every-
body in the Grail community is relieved and relaxed, there is no
reason for playing political games anymore.

There is a celebration. For the second time the Grail is solemnly
brought before the community, especially in honor of Feirefiz and
Parzival's wife Condwiramurs. But let the narrator speak for himself:

> juncfrouwen nu niht langer sint:
> ordenlich si komen über al,
> fünf unt zweinzec an der zal.
> Der ersten blic den heiden clar
> duhte und reideloht ir har,
> die andern schoener aber da nach,
> die er do schierest komen sach,
> unde ir aller kleider tiwer.
> süeze minneclich gehiwer
> was al der meide antlütze gar.
> nah in allen kom diu lieht gevar
> Repanse de schoye, ein magt.
> sich liez der gral, ist mir gesagt,
> die selben tragen eine,
> und anders enkeine.

> [808:28–809:12]

The maidens tarry no longer. In order they came, five-and-twenty in number. The first one struck the heathen as beautiful, and all curls was her
hair. But the ones next following seemed even more beautiful, as he saw
them come in quickly, and all their garments were rich. Sweet, lovable,
and gentle were the faces of all the maidens. Last of all came the radiant
Repanse de Schoye, a virgin. The Grail permitted, I was told, only her to
carry it, no one else. [Mustard/Passage, p. 421]

Whereas the Grail procession during Parzival's first visit showed
an abundance of manipulated eroticism but didn't cause any ques-

tion to be asked, here all erotic features are lacking and questions
are plentiful. The narrator continues first with five indirect questions about descriptions of the Grail festivities, but he dismisses all
of them. Then the Grail begins to provide its riches, but Feirefiz,
being a pagan, cannot see the Grail, although he sees the abundance of food and drinks:

> der heiden *vragte* maere,
> wa von diu goltvaz laere
> vor der tafeln wurden vol.
> daz wundr im tet ze sehen wol.
>
> [810:3–6]

Amfortas asks (!) him whether he sees the Grail in front of him, but
Feirefiz denies it; the only thing he notices is a piece of precious
silk (*achmardi*), on which the Grail rests and which Repanse had
carried into the hall, and in the same breath he confesses that he is
hopelessly in love with her, bursting out in the following questions:

> "waz hilfet al min richheit,
> und swaz ich ie durch wip gestreit,
> und op min hant iht hat vergeben,
> muoz ich sus pinecliche leben?
> ein kreftec got Jupiter,
> waz woltstu min zunsenfte her?"
> minnen kraft mit freuden krenke
> frumt in bleich an siner blenke.
>
> [810:23–30]

"But what good are all my riches, or whatever I have won for women's
sakes, or whatever my hand has bestowed in the way of gifts, if I must live
in such discomfort? My mighty god Jupiter, why hast thou brought me here
for such misery?" Love's power and Joy's weakness made him turn pale in
the white parts of this complexion. [Mustard/Passage, p. 422]

It becomes clear that it is Providence that, although without
erotic prompting, uses Amfortas's political and dynastic scheme,
causing numerous questions to be asked and "prompting" Feirefiz
to fall in love with Queen Repanse, thereby redirecting the future
of the Grail kingdom toward a new, specifically Christian mission.

For soon hereafter Feirefiz is baptized, he marries Repanse, and both depart for India, that is—according to medieval *mappae mundi* —the end of the world in the Orient. Here Repanse gives birth to a son, Prester John, and Christian life, which "was e niht kreftec da" (823:1), is being propagated and strengthened.

Enough about intrigue dynastic and providential, and about *Minne* manipulated and christianized. We must return to the Grail's "despair."

Why was it that Cundrie's accusations were so outrageous when she cursed and condemned Parzival at Arthur's court? It is clear that she as the official messenger of the Grail didn't speak on her own behalf, but appeared as the spokeswoman for the Grail community and especially for King Amfortas. It has also become manifest that the expected visitor was supposed to be the real Red Knight. But as soon as the visitor's armor had been taken away, it became evident that this young man couldn't possibly be the original Red Knight: the young guest was still beardless, his skin probably not pale, his hair certainly not red. We have here another Wolframesque reversal. The mistake was noticed only slowly, probably first by older courtiers who had known the original Red Knight personally. Here the little scene I referred to before becomes fully understandable. The *redespaeher man*, Sir Kay of the Grail court, almost certainly belonged to Amfortas's inner circle and was familiar with the politically motivated prompting scheme that was directed at the Red Knight. When he discovered that the visitor was not the expected real Red Knight, his nerves snapped, and by means of a joke he tried to push the guest in order to get it over with as soon as possible, come what may. Of course, the whole intricate scheme failed. Amfortas and the whole Grail community had to suffer for many more years.[7]

But who had the visitor in the Red Knight's armor been? I could show you how it was Cundrie who found out after some intensive research, but I have to skip this demonstration here. She could not but discover that the guest had been young Parzival, the only possible successor to the Grail kingdom from within the Grail dynasty. And since the Grail community apparently interpreted the message on the Grail as meaning that there was only one opportunity to ask the question, namely during the first night, they could only assume that the tragedy of Amfortas's wounding and impotent rulership would continue—literally into eternity. This would be hell on earth for all concerned. The future would have been so bright *if* Parzival had asked the question!

But a last question has to be stated and answered. How is it possible that Parzival received a second chance? Did the divine power behind the Grail contradict itself? Did mercy prevail over justice? By no means. Since the Grail story is literary fiction of a religious nature, we may expect that the messages appearing on the Grail have some characteristics of an oracle. An oracle has to be interpreted correctly in order to be understood properly. If we read the two statements on the timing of the question again:

> Fragt er niht bi der ersten naht,
> so zerget siner frage maht.

and:

> wirt sin frage an rehter zit getan,
> so sol erz künecriche han,
> unt hat der kumber ende
> von der hohsten hende.

we find that they needn't be understood tautologically but clearly can refer to more than one opportunity or visit, provided that the question is asked during the first night and *an rehter zit*. In other words, the Grail community, immersed as it had been for such a long time in suffering and sadness, was too tense and too preoccupied to see this second interpretation—showing, by the way, *desperatio* in the religious sense, a sin against the Holy Spirit. The narrator hints at this fundamental misunderstanding of the Grail message in a subtle way. Describing ugly Cundrie in book 6 (312: 19–26), he stresses that she is well versed in the liberal arts; but two *artes* are conspicuously missing: music or *harmonia* (which is understandable in view of the desperate Grail court) and *arithmetica*. Cundrie, representative of the Grail community, isn't able to count in a symbolic sense. If she, the Grail community, and especially King Amfortas had been open-minded enough to see the second meaning of the Grail message, too, the manipulation of the procession of the Holy Grail and all the other promptings would have been unnecessary in the first place. Wolfram's *Parzival* shows clearly that God's grace does come, even if late and to slowly wise men.

Hermann J. Weigand, in the new introduction to his book *Wolfram's Parzival: Five Essays*,[8] without being aware of the political games played behind the scenes during Parzival's first visit to the Grail, nevertheless has some very good things to say about Parzival's failure at this first visit:

I have said enough to make it clear that Parzival's failure to inquire of the king regarding his sufferings was not the *cause* of the disastrous consequences. On that night, Parzival, predestined to be king, was not ready to assume his sacred role. He was used by Providence as the catalyst of escalated calamity. The king was not ready for the lifting of the scourge. The Grail company was not ready to be restored to grace. God was not ready to let his wrath be appeased. Parzival was not ready to assume the redeeming function. As the keystone of this analysis let me add: the *story* was not ready for a denouement.[9]

I would like to add two final observations:

It seems to me that politics have not changed much over the centuries. It would pay to look at political configurations in medieval and other literary fiction, especially in works destined for an aristocratic audience, much more carefully. A literary tradition with many fascinating variations might emerge, which would be well deserving of further scrutiny.

Why did Wolfram write his *Parzival*? There are, no doubt, many reasons. I believe that my interpretation has shown an important new aspect. While the German poet's concern for kingship based upon real, albeit often paradoxical, personal experience, particularly in Parzival's case, is clear, the work makes also manifest that kings who play politics in ruthless ways and against divine commands conjure up their own disaster. This is true not only for Amfortas; it applies to a lesser degree to other kings in Wolfram's *Parzival* as well as his *Willehalm*. In the cases of Amfortas and of Loys it is significant that the rulers of the highest kingdoms appear to be most susceptible to the dangers of power, manipulation of others, and isolation from the rest of the world. Such warnings against inordinate politics in Wolfram's works must be heeded. One has no right to expect that Providence is always so full of grace and so divinely patient with slowly wise kings as the divine authority behind the Grail has been with Parzival and the other members of this highest dynasty.

NOTES

1. Because the audience of this paper consisted of a mixture of Arthurian scholars and a generally educated public, I had to give somewhat more details and background material than otherwise might have been necessary. In most places, the style of oral delivery has not been changed. The number of notes has been kept to a minimum. I use the *Parzival* text in Karl Lachmann, ed., *Wolfram von Eschenbach*, 4th ed. (Berlin, 1879); references to the text are given according to stanza and line numbers; the English translations are taken from Helen M. Mustard and Charles E. Passage, transl., *Wolfram von Eschenbach, Parzival. A Romance of the Middle Ages* (New York, 1961), with a few changes. For an up-to-date discussion of almost all the issues touched upon in this paper, see Joachim Bumke, *Die Wolfram von Eschenbach-Forschung seit 1945. Bericht und Bibliographie* (Munich, 1970); the work has a very good index.

2. Cf. Karl Bertau, *Deutsche Literatur im europäischen Mittelalter*, 1: 800–1197 (Munich, 1972), esp. 547–69.

3. "Wolfram von Eschenbach's *Parzival* in the Light of Biblical Typology," *Seminar* 9 (1973): 1–14, esp. 5 f.

4. One notices that the message on the Grail doesn't specify form or content of the question. The Grail, apparently, is generous. If young Parzival had been a little wiser and if he, in his tiredness and embarrassment, had asked something like, "What is this hocus-pocus all about?" he would have saved Amfortas and become king, albeit not a very experienced one.

5. Cf. Percy Ernst Schramm, et al., *Herrschaftszeichen und Staatssymbolik. Beiträge zu ihrer Geschichte vom dritten bis zum sechzehnten Jahrhundert*. 3 vols. (Stuttgart, 1954–56), passim.

6. Cf. 232:11 ff.; 233:4; 234:3 ff.; 235:15 ff.

7. Cf. Weigand's interpretation of this scene in his article, "A Jester at the Grail Castle in Wolfram's *Parzival*?" in Hermann J. Weigand, *Wolfram's Parzival. Five Essays with an Introduction*, edited by Ursula Hoffmann. (Ithaca and London, 1969), pp. 75–119.

8. Cf. ibid.

9. Ibid., p. 15.

III

The Merchant's Tale: *A Tragicomedy of the Neglect of Counsel—The Limits of Art* *

Morton W. Bloomfield
Harvard University

Parody and irony are closely related literary modes, but differ in their manner rather than in their goal. They exist to undermine and undercut the object of their attention. They desire to reduce in some way the object of their attack, to break down the barriers of fixed ideas between and about objects, institutions, persons, and ideas so that we may see them in a different light. Parody is usually active and direct; irony is usually sly and indirect. One is rarely uncertain of the existence of parody—it is open and comic. Of irony one is frequently uncertain. This mode depends on a tone of voice, on exaggeration, on excess, often just a touch of it. A work of art like *The Merchant's Tale*, which heavily indulges in both modes, immediately creates the suspicion that these have something to do with its basic signification. *The Merchant's Tale* is difficult to analyze. As D. S. Brewer writes, "It does not fit into any simple category, its mood is hard to assess, and the daring dislocations of narrative structure . . . have puzzled and sometimes annoyed critics."[1] We should be grateful for whatever clues we can find. A hard look at its parody and irony may lead us to an understanding of at least one of the central themes in the tale.

In its broad outlines the tale illustrates what happens when true counsel (*consilium*) is not followed. *Consilium*, as Aquinas puts it in *De veritate*, quaestio 17, articulus 3, ad 2, is the searching for the proper action and the act of friendly persuasion ("inquisitio de agendis et persuasio amicabilis"), so that the passions of self-love and fleshly appetite may be subordinated to the law of reason and

---

*I am indebted to Miss Patricia Eberle for several very helpful ideas that I have used in the composition of this paper.

the rational love of the common good. When *consilium* lacks or is falsely applied, its proper function of applying the rule of law to the appetites is blocked and the laws of personal and public morality are violated. The initiating action of January, upon which the story is based, is a trespassing of the bonds of moral and divine law. In this case, sexual passion is the villain. In the case of the state, such neglect of *consilium* can be even more disastrous. However, unlike *The Clerk's Tale*, little emphasis in *The Merchant's Tale* is placed upon public violations of counsel. It is the private violation that Chaucer is emphasizing.

Let us turn to the use of parody and irony in this tale, which are basic modes of the narrator. The presence of parody in other tales, such as *The Nun's Priest's Tale*, has been recognized for a very long time. It appears in *The Merchant's Tale* as well, though for some reason scholars and critics have tended to ignore this aspect of the tale—I suspect because the tale itself has tended to be ignored. However, to understand the complexities of this story, the parodic element must not be passed over.

We begin with identifying these parodic elements. They may be classified under various headings—of epic subject matter and style, of courtly love, of classical or ancient history, of courts and rulers, of scholastic reasoning, of romance. The epic parody is most obvi-ous: the address by the narrator to a character when he addresses lovesick Damyan (lines 1866 ff.);[2] apostrophes to Fortune (2057 ff.); epic comparisons, as when the music at the wedding is compared to that of Orpheus, Amphion, Theodamus, and, with a typical medieval mixture of the biblical and classical, Joab (1715 ff.); or as when the narrator compares January's embracing of May to that of Paris and Helen (1752–54); the interference of the gods as in the whole Pluto-Proserpine scene; and so forth. There is a choric ele-ment in the comments of the narrator. In fact, from one rather narrow point of view, *The Merchant's Tale* is a mock epic.

The courtly-love element is presented in the May-January-Damyan triangle. January is the *senex amans*, the *gelos* ("jealous one") of Provençal poetry, the cuckold. He differs from the usual *senex amans* because we are, as we shall see, led to sympathize somewhat with him. He is not like Archambault in the Provençal romance *Flamenca* who is cuckolded by his closely guarded wife and with whom we cannot sympathize. Yet the elaborate pear-tree trick recalls the elaborate scheme of Nicholas in *The Miller's Tale* or Dan John's in *The Shipman's Tale* or Guillaume's in *Flamenca*. The adulterous basis of *The Merchant's Tale* is well founded. Damyan is courtly in his wooing; he appeals for mercy and begs that all be kept secret. He sends and receives secret love letters. In fact the courtly-love element tends to conflict with the fabliau element. The old man is a fabliau figure; the *gelos* is a courtly-love figure. Part of the parody lies in this mixture of themes. Courtly love does not normally appear in conjunction with fabliau tricks except when it is parodied.

Classical machinery and figures are parodied in allusions to Argus (2111), Priapus (2034), Seneca (1376), Cato (1377), and others, some of whom we have alluded to above. Above all, we have the glorious scene between Pluto and Proserpine, who are no more happily married than January and May. Pluto controls Proserpine with the same poor success as January does May. The Bible, especially the Song of Songs, is at least used ironically if not parodied in January's address to May to come into the garden he has built (2138 ff.).

Courts and rulers come in for their share of parody, too. The court flatterer, the "losenger" Placebo, who tells January what he wants to hear, is a classic example of the type. The court of the Lombard knight January, though pleasant in its way, possesses the usual intrigue and flattery we are accustomed to see satirized in works of this sort. Like the king in *Piers Plowman* who must settle the issue between Conscience and Lady Mede, January is set between Justinus and Placebo—except that he is both judge *and* advocate. He neglects or, more properly, misunderstands the proper duty of the ruler: "Wirk alle thyng by conseil" (1485).

In his speech to his friends, when he reveals the depth of his foolishness, with its combination of idealism and delusion, January breaks into scholastic reasoning referring to the causes (more properly, reasons) why a man should marry. These are to have children "by cause of leveful procreacioun" (1448), to avoid the sin of lechery, and finally to create conditions for two people to help each other by living chastely. January, his ridiculousness at its height, repudiates the third "cause." Yet it is he, the pseudoscholastic reasoner, who says, "I counte nat a panyer ful of herbes / Of scole-termes" (1568–69). A further case is given in his speech to his wife as to why she should be faithful to him. He points out (2170 ff.) that she will gain three things thereby—love of Christ, honor to herself, and all his property. The notion of logical if not scholastic argument recalling the *quaestio* runs through the tale—when January worries as to whether if he has bliss on earth he may also have bliss in heaven, when Pluto debates with Proserpine, when May argues January out of the evidence of his eyes after having been caught in flagrante.

As the marriage ceremony is described (1700 ff.), and it is described in some detail, Chaucer slips into the high style of similes, classical and biblical comparisons, astronomical descriptions, personifications and rhetorical *occupatio*. Here we find a parody of that common romance theme, a wedding feast. It is beautifully done and indeed is one of the sources for our knowledge of medieval marriages.

The love situation, as we have said, shares romance and fabliau elements and may be regarded also as parody of romance. The thoughts of the old lover at the feast are a further takeoff on romance heroes in such a situation—a kind of externalized debate of two personifications. The old fool whose appalling if lecherous innocence is now beginning to win us over is kind in his concern for little May who, as he thinks, is about to lose her virginity.

We then meet young Damyan, who falls in love in courtly-love fashion at the sight of fair May. The poet breaks out into a mock apostrophe (1783 ff.) at this point, beginning "O perilous fyr," emphasizing the heinousness of the adder in the bosom.

The lovemaking is described in best romance fashion but alas, without much to report—all from our hero's point of view. Damyan languishes throughout these days but manages to slip his beloved a note, somewhat like Guillaume's using the church service to approach Flamenca.

Chaucer is above all the poet of irony, and in *The Merchant's Tale* he has achieved one of his richest and deepest exemplars.[3] The ironies are many. In the long passage at the beginning praising marriage in ridiculously exaggerated terms (1267–1392), we have irony from the Merchant's point of view but sheer silliness from January's, whose thoughts are presumably being reported here. January speaks of molding young people as "men may warm wex with handes plye" (1430). The only molding in wax is going to be May's molding of the key so that Damyan may later be admitted to the garden. In the same speech January compares himself to a fruit tree (1461 ff.), little dreaming how such a tree is to be his downfall. The Placebo-Justinus debate before January is similarly full of ironies.

We are told too that "love is blynd al day, and may nat see" (1598), and indeed January is to be a living witness to that. January hopes, as the poet of an aubade may hope, that the first night of marriage will last forever (1762–63).[4] We know what a poor performance he is going to put on.

The ironies in the Pluto-Proserpine scene are many—the mixing of biblical, Celtic, and classical lore; the false goddess's (Proserpine) condemning Solomon for making a temple to false gods (2295); the inability of Pluto to control Proserpine's tongue; the parodic nature of the situation in which high (or perhaps low) gods interfere to prevent, as they see it, injustices from being done.[5]

The irony of a woman's loquaciousness that can get her out of anything is also burlesqued. As Rosalind says in *As You Like It*, "You shall never take her [a woman] without her answer unless you take her without her tongue" (Act 4, Scene 1). The irony of January's blindness is clear to our eyes. He is blind when he has his eyes and, as the ending shows, would choose not to see when he has eyes. January believes his wife's lies because he wants to be fooled. He never does face reality, and only in illusion can he be happy. He is the fantasizer par excellence. An act of grace by Pluto does not necessarily produce desirable results, especially as he is hindered by his wife's gift of grace to May—loquacity.

Miss Dempster lists many other examples of irony in the tale, some of which we may here mention. January praises Damyan for the very qualities—secrecy, masculinity, and serviceability—that will enable him to cuckold his master. January sends May to Damyan and begs that she be kind to him. Rebecca is alluded to twice in the tale and she it was who deceived her husband. At his wife's own suggestion, the knight puts his arms around the pear tree to prevent anyone from climbing up it. There are many other touches too, but I think we have presented enough to justify Miss Dempster's opinion that this tale is unique among the *Canterbury Tales* in its extensive use of irony.

The story is told largely from January's point of view. We are strongly made to feel his foolishness at the beginning, but slowly we begin to change. January's thoughtfulness and kindness are suddenly seen. His appeal to his wife to remain loyal to him in his blindness is most touching. Our sympathy for him increases as May's selfishness becomes more and more open. "As the story moves to its ribald denouement, the element of pathos in January's plight stands out in bolder relief and lends him a considerable measure of dignity."[6]

The blindness, helplessness, and affection of the old knight at the end of the tale as he and May go into their palace home out of the garden of delight that he had created and that had stimulated him to greater sexual achievement, create a strong sympathy for this man. He may have been foolish and concupiscent, he may have been morally blind, he may have been a worn-out hulk, but nonetheless most of this is forgotten as we see his plight and even his common humanity in willing not to see what he has seen.

At first we are sorry for poor May, who is married to this foolish old man, but as the story progresses our sympathy vanishes in proportion as it rises for her husband. She is obviously looking for a lover and is only too willing to take on Damyan. She plans her assignation in the pear tree and carries it out even as she hypocritically proclaims her loyalty to her mate. We are not strongly involved with May at the beginning. Her silence is almost complete until nearly the end. It is only then that she talks, an act all the more effective because of her earlier taciturnity, and giving point to Proserpine's gift.

January may well have regarded marriage as licensed sin at the beginning, but he soon learns how unsatisfactory this theory is. He comes to admire May as a person; and although his change of attitude is related to his increasing helplessness, it is not entirely explainable by his sudden blindness, as the fact of his concern just after the marriage ceremony for his sick squire Damyan shows. He is a kindly man in his way, although until then we had not known about it.

In much of the literary criticism of *The Merchant's Tale* for the past thirty-five years, the issue of whether the tale is bitter or not has been the chief bone of contention.[7] Jordan has pointed out that this attitude is the natural outcome of the psychological-dramatic interpretation of the *Canterbury Tales* that has predominated. The Merchant himself is bitter; therefore his tale must be bitter. And evidence for this belief is found, as it may be found for many things when it is sought. The chief piece of evidence is the fact that when the closely guarded May wishes to get rid of Damyan's love note, she tears it up and throws it into the privy. Furthermore, the ironic praise of marriage at the beginning can be interpreted as bitter sarcasm *from the point of view of the Merchant* himself. But the crowning argument is the complaint of the Merchant in his prologue to the tale. This argument assumes that a tale must be read as the expression of a character and that the tales, as Kittredge argued, exist for the sake of the character. This theory is by no means universally accepted.

All this is a rather weak bridge to bear the charges of "unrelieved acidity," "unpitying analysis," "savagely obscene," "frenzy of contempt and hatred"[8] that have been brought against *The Merchant's Tale*. We must add of course what is characteristic of the fabliau genre —successful adultery. It is, however, characteristic of this genre to present an old man cuckolded, and to spend too much time lamenting over his fate is to expect Sophoclean catharsis from Plautine comedies. In fabliaux, husbands get tricked.

The really remarkable thing is that Chaucer does attempt to give us January's point of view and does want us to sympathize with it—or at least to see his dilemma. We cannot call *The Merchant's Tale* a fabliau *tout court* simply because Chaucer does suggest a tragic as well as a romance aspect. It does retain enough of the fabliau element, however, for us to be sure that Chaucer does not want us to concentrate on May's superficial and lustful character.

Chaucer is talking about life in *The Merchant's Tale* and not revealing a bitterness of spirit. He is aware rather of the tragic necessities of life—that one may be more blind spiritually than materially and then, finally, after all learn that perhaps, for certain situations, there are worse things than spiritual blindness—the ability to see clearly. As we have been told, humans can't bear too much reality.

The Merchant's Tale is not a tragedy, of course, but it is a kind of aborted tragedy and if changed in tone could very well have been a true one. But Chaucer wishes only, I think, to suggest tragic possibilities, not to write a tragedy.

The tale is about the transgressing of levels—its comic, romantic, and tragic implications. Before we turn to this subject, let us see how it could have been a tragedy. The tale is a comedy, no doubt, but it is a comedy that carries within it very clearly a *Doppelgänger*—tragedy. It is a comedy that hides a tragedy and that shadows forth a tragedy. Its umbra or anima is tragic. Chaucer, in filling out the fabliau form in this way, makes something new. The French fabliaux may be cruel, but they are also casual. The reader is never allowed to get near enough, as it were, to be seriously involved.[9] But in *The Merchant's Tale*, it is different. The reader is involved. There is, as Burrow says, a generalizing impulse, an attempt to understand, in the tale very foreign to the spirit of the fabliau. The corrosive irony makes us involved willy-nilly.

Tragic too is the great theme of blindness. "The theme of man's tragic blindness pervades Western literature"[10] and is the subject of most tragedies. January is spiritually blind. He treats women as objects. He is not deliberately evil, but limited. His ignoring of true counsel, his lack of knowledge of women, of human relations, of the meaning of love at the beginning—all which may be summed up as his inability to see properly human limits and law—this is his *hamartia*, his fatal weakness, which is responsible for his tragedy. His blindness to the true meaning of his relation to women, his false expectations, his self-delusion, his reliance on poor counsel lead him into a marriage that is bound to fail. Unlike the typical *senex amans*, he is not merely a figure of fun, even at his most foolish moments. We participate from a superior vantage point in his decisions and his debates. Then after the marriage, we gradually see that he has good points. He is thoughtful and kind when his immediate pleasure is not involved. Then lo and behold, he is struck by material, real blindness, an outward manifestation of what was previously inward. We see his increasing helplessness, especially as the relations of May and Damyan become close. We are prepared for the adultery, even the ingeniousness of it.

Fabliau-romance elements struggle with a tragic tale. We are not quite certain what will happen, how January will take it, but

[44]

we know it is coming. An old man married to a beautiful young wife, with a potential lover in the neighborhood, is a setup for a comic triangle, for a prank that will end in bed, with the old man cuckolded. The fabliau conditions are all there. Yet from the beginning this is not a pure fabliau or pure romance. It is not a matter merely of deeper characterization and subtlety of plot. These we can find in *The Miller's Tale*. But it is the wrestling with decisions, with moral problems, the concern with human feelings, with the interior man that make it very different. A man in his blindness is led to his doom, and he begs for a merciful release. We cannot laugh heartily at the old man's discovery. May in ironic and punning words tells him that "He that mysconceyveth, he mysdemeth," and January bows to her reasoning. He had already prepared us for this by the weakening of his argument. When he was granted his sight, he said, "ye algate in it wente! . . . He swyved thee, I saugh it with myne yen" (2376, 2378), but shortly his certainty weakens to "me thoughte" (2386) and "I wende han seyn" (2393). Then finally he becomes spiritually blind again even though he has his eyesight. He is as he was at the beginning: happy in his ignorance.

Burrow calls the anti-fabliau of *The Merchant's Tale* an allegory, and I suppose in the loose sense of the word we may so entitle it. The term refers in his usage to the moral level that is present in the tale. What we have here is a strong conflict between the values of the fabliau with its explicit cynicism and "realism" and those of the tragic "lai" of a type such as Marie de France might have written. This conflict is more basic than the conflict between courtly romance and comedy in the tale. The clash engenders a feeling, abetted by the overwhelming irony of the tale, of having approached a limit in human complexity and of resting in enigmas of the most existentialistic type. The vision of the world presented here is not like that of tragic art with its triumph over death and defeat, nor like that of comedy with its final awareness of human ridiculousness, but rather something partaking of both.

Feeling and ratiocination are set against each other. As Horace Walpole well knew, this means tragedy versus comedy. When you both feel and think about life, you must come to a fundamental antinomy. Chaucer does not take *The Merchant's Tale* to its ultimate limit of silence nor does he transcend its oppositions as he does at the end of *Troilus and Criseyde*, but rather he poses this dilemma and leaves us laughing although with an awareness of how we could cry.

This is a tale of limits and their transgressions. The action begins by January's violating the limits laid down for him by God, nature, and society and ignoring true *consilium* by neglecting rational laws. "Tendre youthe hath wedded stoupyng age" (1738) and a man of high degree has married one "of smal degree" (1625). He has stepped down in the hierarchy of place and has violated the decorum of the universe. At the end, May literally steps over him to violate the limits of moral conduct in her little romp with Damyan. He who had spiritually stepped low to raise up May at the end literally steps low again so that she may ascend even higher. Yet at the end, January is as blind as he was at the beginning. This time he voluntarily chooses blindness because reality is too strong and dazzling for him. If, as F. H. Bradley said, hell is heaven that has come too late, perhaps heaven is a hell that is never perceived. "This Januarie, who is glad but he?" (2412) He rejoices in his voluntary ignorance as he leads his little wife back to their home.

January, after he has married his May and has trespassed through lack of proper counsel the boundaries of age, morality, and class, not to speak of common sense, decides at last, as he settles into his marriage life and as our sympathies for him begin to grow, that he will reintroduce frontiers to protect the boundary of his wife's honor and to enjoy himself within limits by building a walled garden of delight. He tries to recreate boundaries after he has broken them down for his advantage. But the breaker of boundaries has his own boundaries violated in the last scene when both his wall and his wife are penetrated. No limits can protect when the notion of limits is not respected or is misapplied. There is at least a rough working of justice in this world. Those who ignore true counsel pay for it.

January, like the tale about him, has refused to stay within bounds until it is too late. The tale, with its fabliau and anti-fabliau elements, with the gods interfering with human behavior, imitating Christ in conferring grace,[11] going out of their proper bounds (for pagan gods have no right to confer grace), with its walled garden being entered and its privacy shattered, with its constantly shifting style and its parody of style, in short, refuses to be anything and be captured by the reader in boundaries of some sort.

The violation of levels and boundaries in *The Merchant's Tale* is at its most outrageous in the reference to the Wife of Bath by Justinus (1685). This mingling and confusion of two completely different narrative levels wherein a character in a tale refers to one of the pilgrims who is making the journey is unparalleled in all of Chaucer's art as far as I know. It is a bold attack on the proper levels of storytelling and indeed on probability and verisimilitude. It sums up in itself and presents in paradigmatic form the subject of the tale as I see it—the transgression of boundaries. The boundaries between marriage and bachelorhood, between the natural affinity of ages, between gods and men, between pagan and Christian, between men and women, between social ranks, between friends, even between natural sex relations—all these are violated, and above all, generic boundaries are crossed and confused. These violations lead to a comic destructiveness in the tale that critics have mistaken for bitterness. Rather, it is the comedy of the uncontrolled, the comedy of the gratuitous, the comedy of the unlimited.

The whole pear-tree trick is so completely outrageous that it leaves us breathless. The cuckold who provides with his own body the means of his self-deception violates every principle we may hold and reduces the pattern of the universe to sheer unpredictability. It is funny and it violently attacks the probity of woman attempting to prove her complete unscrupulousness. All these events are observed and to some extent controlled by Pluto, who himself earlier had violated the boundary between the human and the divine by stealing Proserpine. Both god and man crossed natural boundaries and both paid for these actions by the continuous presence of the causes of this overstepping: Proserpine and May. Gods need counsel as well as men.

All literary art has a metaquality. It not only communicates a content and a subject but it also communicates itself. A tale is not only about something but it is also about tales. *The Merchant's Tale* tells us the story of a blind old man who is betrayed by his wife, and it also tells us something about such a story and the language it uses. I shall not here discuss the language, what is said about its own language of telling, but I would like to say something about what the tale says about such a story, about itself as a tale.

The Merchant's Tale is partly a tale about how tales can be subversive and destructive and how tales like humans must live within limits. If limits are violated, a tale cannot be unified and present a satisfying perspective on humanity—and cannot indeed finally entertain or teach us. As the host says in the *General Prologue* (line 798), tales should have both *sentence* and *solas*, but when the *solas* fights against the *sentence*, when the amusement is at odds with the morality and vice versa, we are confused. *The Merchant's Tale* is its own critique—and in a sense makes all criticisms superfluous. Its modes of parody and irony break down barriers and make it its own antitale. *The Merchant's Tale* is not a tale of bitterness but a tale of confusion and its consequences. It is at once funny and sad, high and low, up and down—and as in all cases of that sort we are left groping for somewhere to stand. It is about the dangers and humor of not being able to stand properly because we leap over proper barriers or set up false barriers, thereby violating counsel. We laugh while we suppress our desire to cry. It presents itself and a destruction of itself at one and the same time. Yet through blindness one can attain a certain kind of ignorant serenity, as January does at the end of the tale. When barriers are crossed, only blindness can save us from despair. Folly is the unawareness or misconceiving of barriers, and the tale teaches us that only blindness will help the man who will not see or accept the natural limitations of man, of society, and of God.

NOTES

1. In his essay, "The Fabliaux," in *Companion to Chaucer Studies*, ed. Beryl Rowland (Toronto, New York, and London, 1968), p. 260.

2. All references to Chaucer's text are according to F. N. Robinson, ed., *The Works of Geoffrey Chaucer*, 2d ed. (Boston, 1957).

3. For a close study of the many ironies in *The Merchant's Tale*, see Germaine Dempster, *Dramatic Irony in Chaucer*, Stanford University Publications, University Series, Language and Literature 4 (Stanford, 1932), pp. 46 ff. Cf. her statement on p. 58: "His [Chaucer's] success in using the device [irony] with such effectiveness is due largely to the intensity and subtlety of the individual strokes, but even more to their number, to that inexhaustible power of invention which allowed Chaucer to keep up through his long tale the mood of fierce irony so boldly pitched at its highest point in the opening pages—another feature unparalleled in the other works." See also Robert J. Blanch, "Irony in Chaucer's *Merchant's Tale*," *The Lock Haven Review* 8 (1966): 8–15.

4. Cf. *Troilus and Criseyde* 3.1450 ff.

5. For a helpful analysis of the Pluto-Proserpine episode, see Karl P. Wentersdorf, "Theme and Structure in the Merchant's Tale: The Function of the Pluto Episode," *Publications of the Modern Language Association* 80 (1965): 522–27. Wentersdorf shows the relation between this episode and Claudian's *De raptu Proserpinae* (a poem taught in the medieval schools and Chaucer's source for the characters though not the episode).

6. Gertrude M. White, "Hoolynesse or Dotage: The Merchant's January," *Philological Quarterly* 44 (1965): 402. Yet Peter G. Beidler ("Chaucer's Merchant and the Tale of January," *Costerus* 5 [1972]: 2) writes, "January himself comes across as an almost totally unsympathetic character. He is stupid, selfish, and sinful." For January as the type of old age, see Emerson Brown, Jr., "January's 'Unlikely Elde,'" *Neuphilologische Mitteilungen* 74 (1973): 92–106 (not sympathetic to him) and Albert E. Hartung, "The Non-Comic Merchant's Tale, Maximianus, and the Sources," *Mediaeval Studies* 29 (1967): 1–25.

7. On this matter, see Robert M. Jordan, *Chaucer and the Shape of Creation: The Aesthetic Possibilities of Inorganic Structure* (Cambridge, Mass., 1967), pp. 132 ff. (here revising an article published in *Publications of the Modern Language Association* 78 [1963]: 293–99). Cf. also B. H. Bronson, "Afterthoughts on the Merchant's Tale," *Studies in Philology* 57 (1961): 583–96; J. C. McGalliard, "Chaucerian Comedy: The Merchant's Tale, Jonson and Molière," *Philological Quarterly* 25 (1946): 343–70; and Hartung, "The Non-Comic Merchant's Tale," all being opponents of the "bitter" school.

8. Taken from quotations by Tatlock, Kittredge, and Hugh Holman in Jordan, *Chaucer*, pp. 132–33. Dempster, *Dramatic Irony in Chaucer*, and Norman T. Harrington, "Chaucer's *Merchant's Tale*: Another Swing of the Pendulum," *Publications of the Modern Language Association* 86 (1971): 25–31, both support the "bitter" theory. However, although I favor Bronson and Jordan on this point, I do not completely agree with their arguments. With David Shores (*"The Merchant's Tale*. Some Lay Observations," *Neuphilologische Mitteilungen* 71 [1970]: 119–33), I think that *The Merchant's Tale* can be read with the Merchant as narrator without overlaying it with his mood. (See also Mary C. Shroeder, "Fantasy in the *Merchant's Tale*," *Criticism* 12 [1970]: 167–79 on this point.) With Shores also and unlike Jordan, I think the tale more or less unified and not discordant.

9. See J. A. Burrow, "Irony in the Merchant's Tale," *Anglia* 75 (1957): 199. Burrow misinterprets the word "fantasy" in its modern sense. This is, however, a most perceptive article and I am making use of his arguments. Michael D. West ("Drama-

tic Time, Setting, and Motivation in Chaucer," *Chaucer Review* 2 [1967–68]: 172–87)
writes, "The *Merchant's Tale* might be characterized as a fabliau that refuses to stay
within the confines of the fallen world" (p. 173); Malcolm Pittock ("The Merchant's
Tale," *Essays in Criticism* 17 [1967]: 26–40) refers to our tale as an uneasy union of
romance and fabliau (p. 30); and Brewer ("The Fabliaux") sees *The Merchant's Tale* as
"a mixture of courtliness and naturalism."

10. Edward Engelberg, "Tragic Blindness in *The Changeling* and *Women Beware
Women*," *Modern Language Quarterly* 23 (1962): 20.

11. In some of the analogues to the pear-tree tale, Christ himself confers the gift
of sight on the old man. See W. F. Bryan and Germaine Dempster, *Sources and
Analogues of Chaucer's Canterbury Tales* (Chicago, 1941), pp. 341 ff. (in an article by
Dempster).

IV

The Development of a Critical Temper: New Approaches and Modes of Analysis in Fourteenth-Century Philosophy, Science, and Theology

John E. Murdoch
Harvard University

Evaluations of the history of philosophy in the fourteenth century in the Latin West have gradually moved from verdicts claiming it to be a period of skepticism and decline to what many historians now see as more proper views of it as a period of positive philosophical advance. One need not, however, broach the question of the relative merit, or even the usefulness, of these evaluations to realize that one fact is undeniably true: that philosophy in the fourteenth century is markedly different from what one finds in the thirteenth century, a difference that extends to science, medicine, and theology as well. To anyone with even the briefest acquaintance with some of the relevant sources, this difference is intuitively, and immediately, evident. One need only compare, for example, Saint Thomas with William of Ockham, or Siger of Brabant with Jean Buridan, to realize that an important transition has occurred.

It would, of course, be extremely difficult to fix the years of this transition with any precision, but one cannot, I think, doubt that—in the case of most philosophers and theologians—such a transition did occur. It is not so simple, however, to give an adequate account of just what this "shift" consisted in. In fact, it is one stage in my own attempt to give such an account that has provided much of the content of what follows.

To be sure, historians have already addressed themselves to this problem. Ernest Moody has characterized thirteenth-century philosophy as essentially cosmological and speculative in character, that of the fourteenth as basically critical and analytic, while Paul Vignaux has portrayed the difference as one of *"des systèmes"* versus *"des recherches."*[1]

This, however, is but the barest of beginnings, albeit (I believe) an essentially correct one. Admitting that the fourteenth century was fundamentally analytic and critical, it remains to *describe* just how it was so; and, given such a description, to inquire further *how it came to be so*. One should, moreover, ask related questions about the thirteenth century as essentially cosmological and speculative. My own interests center much more on the fourteenth century and, of necessity, on the descriptive phase of the problem. For it is exceedingly problematic to say anything even half definite about the origins of many of the changes that occurred as one moved into the fourteenth century. What is more, that aside, it is better policy to describe these changes with tolerable accuracy before turning to an investigation of how they arose.

My concern with describing the shift that occurred between the thirteenth and fourteenth centuries is, I must confess, very much work in progress.[2] Nevertheless, I have at least one general thesis about this shift that will, I believe, stand relatively untouched as research continues: the most adequate characterization of this shift will be found to derive not from a comparison of content, of particular philosophical or theological conceptions or positions, but rather from an elucidation of differences in *methodology*. This is required for a number of reasons, not the least of them being that, if one operates simply, or even largely, on the basis of specific views or doctrines, one will end up differentiating some particular thinker or thinkers from some particular predecessor or predecessors (Ockham, for example, from Albertus Magnus, or Robert Holcot from Saint Thomas).[3] In order most adequately to describe the transition that occurred between the thirteenth and fourteenth centuries, one should be able to avail oneself of a comparison that will discriminate *most* thinkers in the one century from *most* in the other. (I do not say "all," of course, because there are "static minds" to be found then as well as in any other period.) But given this requirement, I believe that an appropriate cataloging of distinctions in *methodological* factors will move one in the proper direction, namely, that of discriminating "most from most." I intend that "methodological factor" be understood broadly: it includes almost any tool of analysis, any technique of reasoning or of establishing conclusions; and it is also meant to include criteria of certitude and evidence, of what constitutes an effective argument, of what kinds of things are worthy of attention in trying to make a point, and so on.[4]

I should begin by giving some indication of the results I have already reached (and partly published[5]) in unraveling the methodological changes that I feel occurred in the fourteenth century. Let me first set forth two things that all historians consider as being operative in fourteenth-century thought: (1) The repeated invocation of the *potentia Dei absoluta* which—because *this* power of God can bring about anything that does not entail a contradiction—functioned in a purely logical way to expand the investigation of a given problem beyond the physical possibilities operative within (say) Aristotelian physics into the broader area of what was logically permissible.[6] (2) Closely allied with this, the fact that in more instances than not the examination of problems in the fourteenth century proceeded *secundum imaginationem*. Philosophers and theologians repeatedly remind us of the fact that they are reasoning *secundum imaginationem* and appealing to God's absolute power. And they frequently, and appropriately, connect these two factors: God furnishes them a warrant to argue and to make their points *imaginative* as they wished.[7]

Yet once we have come this far, although we have in hand two very central features of fourteenth-century thought, we have not really described as much about its characteristics as might at first sight seem to be the case. For why, one is immediately led to ask, did they come up with *these* particular kinds of *imaginationes* in plying their trade, rather than some others? Now I believe that at least one of the answers to this question is to be found in the fact that the fourteenth century saw the development and application of what I have previously characterized as "new analytical languages" with which to treat both traditional and new problems in philosophy, science, and theology. That is to say, *this* particular *secundum imaginationem* argument occurs and is profitable because it fits with, and is manageable by, this or that "analytical language."

The kinds of languages I have in mind are—to cite but several examples—the language of intension and remission of forms, the language of *incipit* and *desinit* or first and last instants of being or nonbeing, and the theory of supposition.[8] Thus, the language of intension and remission supplied the fourteenth-century scholar with a way of handling or measuring variations in qualities or forms. It allowed him to describe, for example, the distribution of heat throughout a body, whether this distribution was uniform, uniformly nonuniform (in medieval terms, uniformly difform), or nonuniformly nonuniform (difformly difform) from one degree (*gradus*) to another; and even to describe what was involved should it be *imagined* that one such distribution changed into another.[9] The language of *incipit* and *desinit* and the closely related language *de primo et ultimo instanti* afforded ways of ascribing limits to any number of imaginable processes, entities, or events. Thus, for example, if we assume that Socrates is now moving slower than Plato but will increase his velocity such that at some time he will be moving faster than Plato, will there then be a first instant in which Socrates is moving just as fast as or faster than Plato, or a last instant in which he is moving more slowly than Plato?[10] The language or theory of supposition, on the other hand, was one of the keystones of the so-called *logica moderna* of the thirteenth and fourteenth centuries. I shall not attempt even to begin to explain what it meant to the medieval thinker or how it served him.[11] Suffice it to say that supposition dealt with the question of what entity or entities terms within, and only within, propositions stood for (*supponit pro*). Thus, as one of the languages of analysis it served a function that was broader than that of others. For, since the *suppositio* of a given term could vary from one kind of proposition to another, whenever one proposition was proposed as a proper interpretation of another (something that occurred everywhere in philosophy and theology and not just in logic), one had a ready test for this interpretation. If the *suppositio* of a key term in the one proposition differed from its *suppositio* in the other *and* one knew that inference from the one kind of *suppositio* to the other was not valid, then the interpretation was an incorrect, indeed a logically faulty, one.[12]

All of these analytical languages, and others as well, were essentially medieval creations. Some may have been developed out of conceptions or arguments that were found in Aristotle, but anything like their mature form can be found only in the Middle Ages. What is more, although in instances a fair amount of their growth may have occurred in the thirteenth (and even the twelfth) centuries, their wholesale application takes place only in the fourteenth. And it was wholesale. They are found being plied as analytical tools in all corners of philosophy, medicine, and theology. Their applications to problems concerning the human and divine will, to questions of merit and grace, sin and punishment, and to the phenomenon of our love for God and for our fellow creatures were just as respectable and proper as they were to problems of motion, infinite magnitudes or multitudes, and the determination of the effects of drugs in terms of their constituent virtues.[13]

Thus, such languages of analysis gave a kind of unity to philosophical and theological endeavor that was not there before. And because their application is essentially a fourteenth-century preoccupation—one might even say mania—I believe that they are unusually important in describing some of what was involved in the methodological shift that occurred in moving from the thirteenth century into the later Middle Ages.

Now although these analytical languages were impressively pervasive in fourteenth-century thought, they are not the only elements in the methodological shift. Others are broader in scope and (at times) less technical in nature. Some seem simply to have to do with the fact of development within philosophy and theology, with the medieval scholar growing more philosophically mature. The thirteenth-century authors whom we are most apt to have read are already so scholastic and often so Aristotelian that we are inclined to forget the youth of the Aristotelian system in the thirteenth century. Before the century's end it was still relatively new and in the process of being absorbed. Little wonder then that new methodological twists arose as the whole became to be more "under one's belt." Merely to note, for example, how frequently the thirteenth-century treatment of a given issue *begins* from conceptions and doctrines found in the *auctoritates* (Aristotle, Averroes, Peter Lombard, for instance) and is carried out *in terms of* these conceptions and doctrines, while in the fourteenth century investigation of the same issue so often begins from the current *opinio communis* and is carried out in contemporary, not traditional, terms, is surely a methodological difference due to philosophical development or maturation. The order of treatment is also often reversed: the fourteenth-century thinker may well end his analysis by turning to the authoritative position from which the thirteenth-century thinker began.[14]

Other methodological changes that derived from the ordinary and expected course of philosophical development can be seen, I think, in the fact that, given an issue, there was an increasing tendency simultaneously to go beyond the issue or problem to see its connection with other problems or doctrines and at the same time to narrow the problem by singling out what was most crucial to it, by finding a specific subissue or thread that would be especially fruitful in its resolution. The tendency of "going beyond" is found, for example, in the increasing use of analogies and in the constant attention paid to the bearing of logic upon a problem no matter what its original realm.[15] But most striking, I think, is the fact that the technical terminology and conceptual apparatus found in so many thirteenth-century discussions are, even when original and not derived from newly inherited *auctoritates*, much more directly connected to the content of the particular problem under investigation than is the case in the fourteenth century.[16] Then the technical baggage is far more likely to be methodological and not tied to the problem at hand. It may be, for example, part and parcel of some given analytical language that is being applied.[17] But this expands the problem by connecting it, even if only methodologically, with others—others that will turn out to be of the same type and hence potentially illuminating for the matter at hand.[18]

On the other hand, as one moves toward and into the fourteenth century, problems are narrowed in the sense that the kinds of material treated in the resolution of a problem often become less comprehensive. This narrowing seems in general related to a greater awareness and a spelling out of just which assumptions are at stake in a problem and its resolution. The *determinatio* of a given question increasingly finds itself stocked with the systematic display of needed *definitiones*, *distinctiones*, *notabilia*, *suppositiones*, and other *praemittenda*. And from these, of course, there follow, in equally systematic fashion, the appropriate bevy of *conclusiones*.[19]

Alternatively, the compass of a problem is narrowed when some particular subissue or implication comes to be regarded as the central core of that under investigation. Thus, St. Bonaventure discusses the eternity of the world in such a way as to make it appear that the nub of the problem should be seen in the absurdities it entails with respect to the infinite.[20] Whether he intended it or not, subsequent thinkers, especially fourteenth-century ones, emphasized and developed this relevance of the infinite to eternity, at times almost to the exclusion of everything else.[21] The infinite also became the crucial element in the discussion of God's omnipotence, the continuity of motion became central to the determination of how angels proceeded from place to place, and the nature of *relationes* was frequently taken to be one of the more important aspects in discussing the Trinity.[22] Similarly, one might come to believe that the best way to treat the question of whether motion was some kind of entity beyond the bodies undergoing motion and the places between which they moved was not to approach motion itself, but to concentrate attention upon the *impulsus* or *inclinationes* involved in motion or even solely upon the *continuitas* it necessarily possessed.[23]

What is more, this simultaneous expanding and narrowing of a problem often led to a change in the face of the very problem itself. Discussions of angelic motion turned into veritable disquisitions on the problem of the continuum and not much else. Scarcely an angel is mentioned.[24] Even more noticeable is the evolution of the infinite and the eternity of the world: succinctly put, the eternity of the world simply drops from view, while precisely the same issues of infinity to which it had given rise carry on a life of their own. Other ways are found to generate the same considerations relative to the infinite: whatever infinite task can be accomplished given an eternity, let God do the same in one hour; or simply appeal to his omniscience as capable of knowing determinately the infinites that are so beyond us.[25] Once this becomes habit, the same things are often assumed as done without even mentioning God.[26] Perhaps it was taken as understood.

I have tried to ascribe the changes in the way problems were treated to nothing more than the natural development of philosophy. But perhaps some of them are more connected than I have implied to the appearance of specific philosophical methods or po-

sitions in the fourteenth century. They might, for example, be con-
comitants of the developing analytical languages of which I spoke
earlier. However, I presently have in mind a more singular doctrine
or position—the "particularism" associated with William of Ockham but maintained by any number of other fourteenth-century
scholars as well: only individual *res permanentes* exist; only individual substances and instances of qualities.[27] This particularism is
surely behind the transformation of the (thirteenth-century) question of in what categories motion is to be found into the (fourteenth-
century) question of whether it is a thing distinct from individual
res permanentes.[28] And in Ockham himself it is probably connected
with his predilection to give general arguments second or last and
to have his appeals to the *potentia Dei absoluta* refer so often to individual, concrete things.[29] But the relation is perhaps even deeper.
Can one not reasonably claim that particularism is related not merely to the fact that motion, for example, is examined in terms of
individual mobiles, but also to the fact that individual *kinds* of
motion within individual mobiles are treated with increasing fre-
quency?[30]

   On the other hand, particularism had its problems as well as
(from our point of view perhaps) its virtues. For if all we have are
individual *res permanentes*—individual mobiles, individual places,
individual heats, and individual sizes, for example—then we can
really say very little of what we would like about motion. Motion is
a successive, not a permanent, thing and we should be able to talk
about that. It is also in most instances continuous and can be found
in various speeds, and we should be able to give accounts of such
things as well. However, the nonparticularist would claim, one
cannot do so simply with *res permanentes* at one's disposal.[31] Yet
that was not the only difficulty. Individuals and events involving
individuals are absolutely contingent (they can be or they can not
be); but if we should wish to have a *scientia demonstrativa* dealing
with (again, for example) motion, this will not do, since any such
scientia must deal with universal and necessary, not contingent,
things. The particularist replied to both of these difficulties in one
fell swoop. One had merely to shift things to the *vehicles* for trans-
mitting knowledge about motion, that is, to the *propositiones* or
complexa that speak about motion, mobiles, etc. This not only re-

solved the two difficulties laid at the door of a particularist ontology but had other advantages as well. *Scientia* consists in nothing more than *propositiones* in the first place, and—at least for some particularists—they are the only things that can properly be said to be true.[32] In the bargain one will automatically derive the universality and necessity required for *scientia*.[33] We can also, for example, say all we need to about motion, since the multiplicity required to explain the successiveness, continuity, and velocities involved in motion exists on the level of language, of propositions, while unity is preserved on the level of things.[34]

The examples I have drawn from Ockham's discussion of motion are, moreover, but particular instances of a much more widespread phenomenon: the tendency to analyze almost any problem metalinguistically. In place of speaking directly about the events or entities relevant to a given problem, one analyzed matters by operating with and upon the propositions and terms within propositions that stood for, respectively, those events or entities. One had to do with what one might term *propositional analysis* or, to put it in a more medieval way, one examined things from a "second intentional" point of view.[35] Inasmuch as this propositional approach to problems is so prevalent, it is well worth closer examination. Of course, the use I have already cited of the theory of supposition as an analytical language is a case of such propositional analysis. As a case it goes back well into the thirteenth century,[36] but it is really the fourteenth century that is witness to its flourishing and to the development and widespread use of all other manners of propositional analysis as well.

At times one is explicitly told that logic and such analysis are being brought to bear upon problems in natural philosophy. Thus, John the Canon troubles to set out verbatim the rule of supposition theory that he will apply in his discussion of continuous quantities.[37] Or Walter Burley tells us that his account of *suppositio* will "resolve difficulties that occur in natural philosophy (*in scientia naturali*) and in other *scientia*," difficulties that "are due to an ignorance" of what he has just set forth.[38] In other instances, the introduction of propositional analysis is more subtle. Hence, Robert Holcot prepares his discussion of the eternity of the world for such an analysis by announcing the *questio* itself in terms of God's knowledge of his creation, a knowledge that of necessity is based upon propositions and, at one and the same time, allows him to introduce a number of other issues for "propositional" treatment.[39] In another passage he opens his criticism of Anselm's ontological argument with the words: "Tu audis istum terminum: 'istud quo maius cogitari non potest.'" Now, he adds, "either you understand what you hear or you do not," which leads him directly to a propositional analysis of the *terminus* that is at the heart of Anselm's argument.[40]

It would be all but impossible at this point even to catalog the kinds of propositional analysis that occur throughout fourteenth-century philosophy and theology. Some of the more common take events or entities that presumably involve necessity or possibility and reduce them to the relevant modalities of propositions;[41] others attempt to apply "tense logic" to truths about past or future events.[42]

But a more adequate notion of what is involved can be had if several examples are examined at closer hand. Once again, let me cite Ockham and the problem of motion. In his view, remember, the problem asks whether motion involves any entity above and beyond individual *res permanentes*. He gives two separate analyses of the problem, the first early in his career in his commentary on Lombard's *Sentences*. What he here claims at first sight sounds most peculiar: "It is evident that motion is composed of affirmations —for instance, out of the parts acquired by motion—and negations of the other following parts (which are infinite in number)."[43] Without quoting more from his exposition, what he has in mind by these "affirmations" and "negations" are propositions: affirmative propositions asserting that so much heat (for example) has been acquired or so much space has been traversed, by a given mobile; and negative propositions denying that these further parts of heat or space have been acquired or traversed by the mobile. The negative propositions are especially important; they are required, he tells us, "because motion necessarily includes succession."[44] That is to say, when one has but a *res permanentes* ontology, negative statements telling what the permanent entity or mobile has *not* done are needed because then "no entity aside from permanent things (that is, the mobile and the places it successively occupies) is assumed to exist."[45]

In his more mature treatment of motion in his *Expositio super libros physicorum*[46] Ockham refers to his earlier view of motion as composed of affirmations and negations,[47] but proposes a quite different, more satisfactory, propositional analysis of the problem. In essence, his proposal is that the noun *motion* is an abstract, connotative term and we should therefore reduce any proposition in which it occurs to a proposition, or set of propositions, that contain only "absolute terms," since such terms refer, and only refer, to individual, concrete *res permanentes*. That is, with such reductions everywhere made, one can say all one wishes about motion and still preserve a particularist ontology (nothing but individual mobiles and individual places to be occupied).[48] Ockham's razor has been wielded. In his specific arguments he shows that the procedure to be followed in answering questions about motion is always, in effect, based on a consideration of the properties of the kinds of terms and propositions we must utilize in framing these answers.[49] The analysis is thoroughly propositional. Should there be any doubt, Ockham erases it with what (by fourteenth-century standards) is an especially happy and succinct passage telling us what it is all about:

An abstract noun fiction constructed out of adverbs, conjunctions, prepositions, verbs, and syncategorematic terms causes many difficulties and leads many into error. For many thinkers imagine that just as there are distinct nouns there are distinct things corresponding to them, so that insofar as there is a distinction between things signified, to such an extent there is a distinction between the signifying nouns. This, however, is not true. For sometimes the same things are signified when there is a difference in the logical or grammatical manner of signifying. . . . Thus, in modern times, because of the errors arising from the use of such abstract nouns, it would be better in philosophy, for the sake of simplicity, not to use them but only the verbs, adverbs, conjunctions, prepositions, and syncategorematic terms as they were instituted in the first place. This is preferable to the invention of such abstract nouns and their use. Indeed, were it not for the use of such abstract terms as "motion," "mutation," "mutability," "simultaneity," "succession," "rest," and the like, there would be little difficulty with respect to motion, mutation, time, instants, and so forth.[50]

This is only one manner in which Ockham brings propositional analysis to bear upon the investigation of problems. Others are quite different. In his criticism of Duns Scotus's doctrine of divine infinity, for example, he accurately reformulates Scotus's argument establishing that the most eminent being must be infinite, but then, taking another argument that is propositionally identical with that given by Scotus (albeit totally different in content), Ockham shows that, just as his alternative argument is invalid, so is that of Scotus. Ockham makes his point not by a conceptual analysis of divine infinity, but rather by an examination of the modal propositions that Scotus had employed to prove his contention of divine infinity.[51] This is but another form of propositional analysis.

In Ockham's eyes such an approach was everywhere legitimate and productive. It could be, and was, brought to bear in the resolution of all manner of problems, in the criticism of the contentions of contemporaries, and even in the interpretation of *antiqui* such as Aristotle. In such instances, Ockham at times recognized that this type of analysis was not that practiced by the Philosopher, but he was quick to add that it did not falsify or misrepresent what Aristotle had in mind, and in fact was but a more adequate way of explaining what he did mean.[52] That is to say, because propositional analysis was basically a methodological innovation, it did not dictate, or even affect, results or content.

I have quoted most extensively from Ockham, but this must in no way lead to the belief that propositional analysis, even extended propositional analysis, was somehow a semiexclusive commodity belonging to him or even to him together with his followers. Quite the contrary; it appears throughout fourteenth-century philosophy and theology in the works of those who disagree with Ockham in numerous ways[53] and can even be found in one of his immediate opponents concerning his views on motion, a case in which, as we have seen, its application was particularly "thick" in what Ockham had to say.[54] Propositional analysis is, then, an important characteristic of the fourteenth century as a whole.

This kind of approach to problems was, of course, very much part of the yield given by medieval logic to the area of new methods of analysis. But logic contributed to the techniques of investigating philosophical and theological questions in any number of other ways. One of them concerned mathematics, and care must be taken to elucidate just how much of the contribution was mathematical and how much was logical. Fundamentally, the issue was one of the function and scope of axioms or *prima principia* within a systematic presentation of geometry like Euclid's *Elements*. Curiously enough, this issue was attacked not when doing or examining some body of knowledge or discipline that was similar to Euclid's (or any Greek) mathematics; it occurred instead when dealing with such un-Greek ideas as the mathematics of the infinite or of indivisibles. Thus, it was asked whether or not the usual axioms found in Euclid as applied to finite magnitudes could be properly applied in the case of infinite ones. The beginning of such questions can be found in the later thirteenth century,[55] but it is only in the fourteenth that one finds their treatment becoming substantially productive,[56] so productive in fact that, in at least one instance, a proper understanding of the mathematics of the infinite does indeed result.[57]

No less impressive is an alternative way in which the role of mathematical *prima principia* were viewed, an alternative that approached the whole issue from another direction. One of its most penetrating instances occurs in Thomas Bradwardine's *Tractatus de continuo*, a treatise written in axiomatic fashion whose primary burden was to champion Aristotle's view of continuous quantities and to lay to rest once and for all any contention that such quantities could be composed of indivisibles. His refutation of such contentions proceeded almost totally on the basis of geometry,[58] but at its end he astutely asked the question of just which "axioms" concerning the composition of continua is geometry based on in the first place. Perhaps, in relying so heavily on geometry in his refutation, he had begged the whole question! Not so, he replies, for one *can* allow the composition of magnitudes out of indivisibles of a certain sort and prove all of the standard theorems of geometry nonetheless.[59] What he has done is to probe the logic of assumptions made in mathematics and (in modern terms) broach the question of just which axioms were independent of this system of geometry as he knew it and which were not.[60]

It is an intriguing question whether his ability to realize the importance of such a consideration, or the abilities of others to see the significance of certain axioms to an understanding of the infinite, was based more on a familiarity with medieval mathematics or upon an extensive exposure to medieval logic. Perhaps these two alternatives should not be considered as influences or backgrounds as distinct as we might initially think. For when one looks carefully at the medieval Euclid, and particularly at what was written in the margins by its thirteenth- and fourteenth-century readers, it becomes apparent that one of the major things medievals found of interest in Euclid was what it enabled them to learn of the logic of an axiomatic system.[61] What could be more natural for a geometry studied in a medieval faculty of arts where, as a discipline, logic was so supremely prevalent, perhaps in some ways even dominant?

Still, in whatever way one should measure the extent of its presence, there is no doubt that logic contributed to precisely how the fourteenth century was analytic in yet another fashion: the contribution was the tradition of sophismata. Unfortunately, any attempt to explain just what sophisms were in the Middle Ages is made more difficult than necessary by the fact that the term *sophism* was used to mean a fair number of different things.[62] For present purposes I have in mind a particular group of things that received this label, the most important group, I believe, constituting as it did a significant segment of the medieval logical tradition. Omitting any number of qualifications that would be required were one to examine in any depth the meaning of even this important and predominant class of sophismata, it is sufficient to begin by noting that the sophism itself was simply a statement or proposition that was most frequently rather striking in its bizarreness. Typical examples are *Omnis homo est omnis homo; Deus scit quicquid scivit; Nichil et chimera sunt fratres; Infinita sunt finita; Cuiuslibet hominis asinus currit; Nullo homine currente, tu es asinus; Omnes homines sunt asini vel homines et asini sunt asini.*[63]

Yet these are only the sophisms themselves. Their true importance lies in the function they served, first in logic and grammar and then later (in the fourteenth century) in natural philosophy. If one concentrates initially on the role they played within the standard logical texts of the thirteenth century (Peter of Spain and William of Sherwood, for instance), it is apparent that they most frequently served as examples designed to help explain or confirm logical rules. The rule might state an ambiguity or a clear-cut distinction, or might deny that an inference can be made under such and such circumstances, the sophism then either illustrating the distinction or ambiguity in a rather graphic way or showing what would occur if the forbidden inference were made.[64] This is at least one of the functions sophismata served within standard logical texts. But there soon arose rather substantial collections of nothing but sophismata, first in the thirteenth century in logic, and then in the fourteenth century partly in natural philosophy as well.[65] What function did they have then? They no longer appeared as appendages to specific logical rules they were intended to illustrate. Still, their function was similar, but more advanced, more comprehensive. These collections served, I believe, as something like handbooks, in which the emphasis was upon learning how to apply and operate with any number of logical—or, alternatively, natural philosophical—techniques, rules, or conceptions. The purpose was to become as adept as possible in utilizing these techniques to solve any number of problems (here termed *sophisms*), the problems in and of themselves being of no special importance.[66] In the fourteenth century these handbooks or, more often than that, separate sophisms of a considerable length and complexity, increased markedly in popularity. And why not? They fit so well with the analytic penchant. They furnished a ready and convenient way one could learn not just the fine points of logic, but develop an expertise in applying the various analytical languages in philosophy and theology as well.[67] They too, then, help in explaining just how the fourteenth century was analytic.[68]

Thus far I have spent almost every word attempting to reveal at least some of the ways in which the fourteenth century parted ways with the thirteenth and replaced the speculative system building of the latter with an analytic approach. But the overall characterization with which I began claimed that it was critical as well. A few words should be devoted to that also. The first thing that comes to mind is the criticism of Aristotle (and other authorities) that is spoken of by historians as being so much part of the fourteenth century. Although it is true that he was criticized, one should be clear about just what this criticism consisted in. It was never predominantly concerned with the fact that his doctrines and conceptions did not fit the facts or did not adequately "save the phenomena." It was much more a case of finding out Aristotle's precise intentions and of rendering his arguments and conceptions more rigorous, an increased rigor that was in many instances established by rephrasing or reinterpreting Aristotle in such a way as to make him consistent with new, fourteenth-century philosophical and methodological demands.[69]

Yet the fourteenth century was critical in smaller, but perhaps equally significant, ways as well. There is considerable evidence of a tendency, for example, to refrain from attempting to render a definitive decision concerning competing conceptions or theories, the emphasis instead falling on how many points, conclusions, or arguments can be drawn from these theories, the longer and more complex one's final inventory the better. One of the most striking examples of such a tendency is the *Liber calculationum* of Richard Swineshead and some of the works of his Mertonian colleagues.[70] But what looks like indecisiveness is broader than that. At times there appears to be as much interest in generating objections as in resolving them.[71] At other times, views are held more because of the critical weight of the opposing *opinio* than because of the positive weight on the side being adhered to.[72] And similar attitudes are found in theology as well as philosophy. Elaborate theories are formulated to deal with such issues as the perfections of species and in the final analysis apparently abandoned as inadequate.[73] It would seem that the value and interest of these theories lay simply in their formulation. Similarly, substantial digressions are inserted into theological contexts and the claim (or excuse) is made that the author is writing or inquiring *curiose*.[74] These things too are, I think, either evidence for, or results of, a critical attitude.

Those of you here whose bailiwick is the very late Middle Ages or the Renaissance itself, will have recognized that, in large measure, it was exactly those features of fourteenth-century thought that I have delineated as describing how this thought was analytic and critical that in the years to come brought not too few humanists to the very brink of apoplexy. For many of the protagonists in the plot I have tried to trace were the *barbari Britanni* who so exercised the likes of Coluccio Salutati and, for Leonardo Bruni, were those *quorum etiam nomina perhorresco.*[75] There were, however, if not dyed-in-the-wool humanists, at least literary figures who viewed these fourteenth-century accomplishments without such disdain or complaint. They were at least aware of some of the content of the analytic tradition. Partly as information, but perhaps more in honor of the more literary part of the present institute, I should like to close by reading a few lines from the *Court of Sapience*, a fifteenth-century Middle English poem once erroneously attributed to John Lydgate. In a tour of the Castle of Knowledge, visit is appropriately paid to the apartments of each of the seven liberal arts. We enter that of Dame Dialectica:

> Her parlour fresshe, hyr clothyng prowde and stoute,
> Of "differt," "scire" and of "incipit,"
> Wyth sophyms full depeyntyd was aboute,
> And other matiers as of "desinit";
> The comone tretyse taught she theym therwyth:
> Whiche [ys] quatkyn, what hys proporcioun
> What thyng he ys and hys divisioun. . . .
> She taught theym there, wyth lust and all lykyng;
> Fast they dispute[n] in theyr comonyng,
> Wyth sophyms strong straunge matyers they dyscus,
> And fast they cry oft: "Tu es asinus."[76]

I seriously doubt that the author of the poem really understood the "mysteries" of sophismata and *de incipit et desinit*, but the elements are there.[77] He is witness to at least part of what the whole analytic attitude was all about. And to find this in a poem rather than in a text of logic or a commentary on Aristotle's *Physics* encourages me further in my belief that a very central feature of this attitude really was like that.

NOTES

1. Ernest Moody, "Empiricism and Metaphysics in Medieval Philosophy," *Philosophical Review* 67 (1958): 161. Paul Vignaux's characterization was made orally in his comments during a symposium on "The Conception of Philosophy in the Middle Ages" (the lead paper being given by F. Van Steenberghen), held during the Fifth International Congress of Medieval Philosophy in Madrid, September 1972.

2. Some of this work has appeared in print (see the articles referred to in nn. 5, 37, and 68, in particular), but much more is still truly "in the making." I have approached the problem in two different ways: first, by examining the appearance of new modes of analysis and argument in a great variety of corners and questions of late medieval philosophy and theology; second, by tracing the treatment of a given topic as one proceeds from the thirteenth to the fourteenth century. Both of these approaches are represented in what follows, but the latter is more predominant. I have in particular drawn upon the comparative treatment of the topics of the nature of motion, the eternity of the world, and the analysis of continuity and infinity. I have here benefited from seminars given at Harvard and, most recently, at this very institute this summer; in terms of new thoughts and stimulus, much of the "ex quo" of what follows is owed to these occasions.

3. This is why attempts to describe nominalism or to decide which fourteenth-century figures were nominalists and in what sense are helpful but not adequate for the kind of differentiation I have in mind. Two "chroniques" of such attempts have recently been published by William Courtenay: "Nominalism and Late Medieval Thought: A Bibliographical Essay," *Theological Studies* 33 (1972): 716–34; "Nominalism and Late Medieval Religion," in *The Pursuit of Holiness in Late Medieval and Renaissance Religion*, ed. Charles Trinkhaus and Heiko A. Oberman (Leiden, 1974), pp. 26–59.

4. This naturally makes my exposition doubly difficult. Not only is the content of thirteenth- and fourteenth-century philosophy extraordinarily complex and technical, but I will be trying to direct attention to *how* this content is treated without mentioning much of it.

5. J. E. Murdoch, "From Social into Intellectual Factors: An Aspect of the Unitary Character of Late Medieval Learning," in *The Cultural Context of Medieval Learning*, ed. J. E. Murdoch and E. D. Sylla (Dordrecht, 1975), pp. 271–339. Logically these results should perhaps come at some later stage in a description of the differences between the thirteenth and fourteenth centuries, but since I have found myself working on them first, perhaps this violence against good order might be excused.

6. This way of putting the role of God's *potentia absoluta* ignores a number of aspects of the "dialectics of God's powers" that are important within theology (see, for example, Heiko Oberman, *The Harvest of Medieval Theology. Gabriel Biel and Late Medieval Nominalism* [Cambridge, Mass., 1963], chap. 2), but this is far and away the function it most frequently played within natural philosophy. A particularly instructive example of the "logical force" of the *potentia absoluta* in this regard can be derived from comparing Aristotle's extensive, but largely *physical*, analysis of the infinite (*Phys.* 3, chaps. 4–8 and *De caelo* 1, chaps. 5–7) with the late medieval investigation of whether, and what kind of, infinity is *logically* possible (an investigation frequently approached by asking *utrum Deus possit facere magnitudinem [sive multitudinem] in actu*; the *locus classicus* for this question is book 1, dist. 43 of commentaries on Peter Lombard's *Sentences*).

7. Thus, for example, Richard Fitzralph, *Comm. Sent.* lib. 2, quaest. 1, art. 1 (*Utrum includat contradictionem Deum produxisse mundum ab eterno*) explicitly claims that "Deus potest facere quidquid creatura potest ymaginari fieri"; or less generally: "quod quidquid potest ymaginari creatura facere in tempore finito potest Deus

facere in instanti" (MS Paris, BN lat. 15853, fol. 140r–v). A rather unusual way of expressing the nature and force of *imaginatio* is found in Walter Chatton (?) who, when speaking of the infinite divisibility of a quantity, allows that "infinite partes esse proportionales tantum in ymaginatione (que est impossibilium) et non experitur homo se cessare ymaginando nisi ad imperium voluntatis," but then rejects such an infinity of parts "quia ymaginata non sunt partes rei" (see J. E. Murdoch and E. Synan, "Two Questions on the Continuum: Walter Chatton (?), O.F.M. and Adam Wodeham, O.F.M.," *Franciscan Studies* 26 [1966]: 235). But this kind of specification of the irrelevance of *secundum imaginationem* considerations is not frequently encountered, at least not so explicitly.

8. To refer to all of these simply as "analytical languages" without further qualification glosses over important distinctions. Thus, to cite one of the most significant, *suppositio* was a "metalanguage" dealing as it did with propositions and their terms, to be distinguished from the likes of the "languages" of intension and remission or first and last instants whose statements or rules were expressed in what we would now term the object language. But this difference does not alter the point I wish to make about the importance of fourteenth-century thought. A more complete exposition of what was involved in these late medieval analytical languages can be found in Murdoch, "From Social into Intellectual Factors," pp. 280–89.

9. To be sure, not all possible distributions of a quality, or all possible changes of one distribution into another, could be, or were, considered by fourteenth-century thinkers. Only those cases that were "manageable," cases that could be expressed and analyzed by the logical and mathematical techniques at their disposal, were treated. But the level of complexity and sophistication that was reached is by no means insignificant or unimpressive, especially in the works of such figures as Richard Swineshead (see the article of J. E. Murdoch and E. D. Sylla in the *Dictionary of Scientific Biography* [New York, 1976], 13:184–213) and Nicole Oresme (see Marshall Clagett, *Nicole Oresme and the Medieval Geometry of Qualities and Motions* [Madison, 1968]).

10. This particular example is an artificial one, but it encapsulates the substance of what one finds in the likes of William Heytesbury and Richard Killington. See Curtis Wilson, *William Heytesbury: Medieval Logic and the Rise of Mathematical Physics* (Madison, 1956), pp. 29–56, 163–68.

11. On *suppositio* in the later Middle Ages, see William Kneale and Martha Kneale, *The Development of Logic* (Oxford, 1962), pp. 246–74; Ernest Moody, *Truth and Consequence in Mediaeval Logic* (Amsterdam, 1953), chaps. 1–3; Philotheus Boehner, *Collected Articles on Ockham* (St. Bonaventure, N.Y., 1958), pp. 174–267.

12. Of course, if the inference in question was valid, this did not mean that the interpretation was a good or informative one. Cf. Murdoch, "From Social into Intellectual Factors," p. 319, n. 63.

13. For the theological applications see ibid., pp. 289–97; for the pharmacological applications see Michael McVaugh, "Arnald of Villanova and Bradwardine's Law," *Isis* 58 (1967): 56–64, and "Quantified Medical Theory and Practice at Fourteenth-Century Montpellier," *Bulletin of the History of Medicine* 43 (1969): 397–413.

14. Thus, Albertus Magnus (*Physicorum*, lib. 3, tract. 1, cap. 3 [*Opera*, vol. 3, ed. Borgnet, pp. 181–90]) begins his analysis of the proper genus of motion from the material he finds in Avicenna and Averroes and carries it out largely in terms of this material, while William of Ockham (*Tractatus de successivis*, ed. P. Boehner [St. Bonaventure, N.Y., 1944], pp. 32–69) may mention the relevant passage of Averroes at the beginning of his analysis of motion, but he treats the issues presented by Averroes only *after* he has carried out his analysis in his own terms.

15. An especially illuminating case of applying logic to something that, prima facie, might be considered outside its realm is that of the infinite. See, for example, Peter of Spain, *Tractatus, called afterwards Summule logicales*, ed. L. M. De Rijk (Assen,

1972), pp. 230–32; William of Sherwood, *Treatise on Syncategorematic Terms*, trans. Norman Kretzmann (Minneapolis, 1968), pp. 41–43; William Heytesbury, *Sophismata* (ed. Venice, 1494), fols. 130v–134r. All of these texts treat of the sophism *Infinita sunt finita*, on which see E. D. Sylla, "Medieval Logic and the Infinite," *XIVth International Congress of the History of Science, Proceedings No. 2* (Tokyo, 1975), pp. 87–91. Application of logic to the infinite that does not involve this sophism can be seen, for example, in William of Alnwick, *Determinatio 2* (MS Vatican, Pal. lat. 1805, fol. 10r):

Dicendum quod omne tempus excessum a tempore infinito est finitum, quoniam quelibet singularis est vera, et etiam sua contradictoria est falsa. Et concedendum quod totum tempus finitum exceditur a tempore infinito. Sed non sequitur quod tantum sive precise hoc aut illud totale tempus sit excessum a tempore infinito, quoniam a superiori ad inferius non tenet consequentia cum dictione exclusiva a parte subiecti. Sicud non sequitur: "Tantum animal est homo, igitur tantum hoc animal aut illud est homo"; sicut et non sequitur: "Tantum numerus finitus exceditur a multitudine infinita, igitur tantum hic numerus aut ille exceditur a multitudine infinita." . . . Dicendum quod in ista: "Omnia tempora excessa a tempore infinito sunt finita," "omnia" potest teneri distributive, et sic verum est quod sunt finita, quia quodlibet eorum est finitum. Si autem teneatur collective, sic includentur incompossibilia ex parte subiecti, scilicet quod omnia tempora collective accepta sint excessa a tempore finito.

16. For example, the key operative terms in Albertus Magnus's analysis of motion (above, n. 14) are the likes of *fluxus; ens, ubi,* or *forma fluens; via; forma permixta potentie, forma que est actus materie,* and *forma que est potentia in materia*—all of which are directly and intimately connected with the Aristotelian conception of motion. Albertus derived the better part of these technical terms from Averroes and Avicenna. That these particular terms are far from incidental to his discussion is evident from the fact that they are at the very basis of his determination of whether or not, and in what sense, a motion is essentially identical with, but existentially distinct from, the terminus toward which it tends. If essentially identical, then the motion in question belongs to the same genus or category as its terminus and there are as many genera of motion as there are of termini; if not, then motion might be considered to belong to a genus of its own. But this question of the genera or genus of motion is the whole problem of motion to which Albertus was addressing himself (*Qualiter motus cadit in predicamento*).

17. As we shall see in what follows, William of Ockham's analysis of motion proceeds essentially by focusing attention upon the terms and propositions utilized in speaking of motion and, as such, his technical terminology derives from logic and not from those conceptions and doctrines traditionally utilized in defining and dealing with motion. Similarly, although he disagrees with Ockham's view when it comes to local motion, Jean Buridan utilized such logical apparatus as the theory of *suppositio* and the notion of *differentia nominis* when he decided that motion of alteration is not distinct *ab alterabili et qualitate secundum quam est alteratio* (*Questiones super octo physicorum libros,* ed. Paris, 1509: lib. 3, quaest. 2; fol. 42r–v). An example of the utilization of a technical vocabulary belonging to a new "analytical language" that is itself more tied to *motus* (taken in its broadest sense) can be found in John Dumbleton. In his investigation of the *quid* and *qualia* of motion in his *Summa logicalium et naturalium,* pars 3, cap. 26–31 (MS Cambridge, Peterhouse 272, fols. 29r–31r) he appeals repeatedly to *intensio, latitudo, distantia qualitativa, gradus, proportiones,* etc., as key technical terms. Yet even though we here have a terminology that is indeed more related to *motus* than in the case of someone like Ockham, it is not as specifically connected with motion as that employed by Albertus Magnus. Dumbleton's "analytical languages" have roots in medicine and most probably such things as the investigation of light, and they are being simultaneously utilized

to cover problems in philosophy and theology that have little, if anything, to do with motion. On all of this, see these two articles of E. D. Sylla: "Medieval Quantifications of Qualities: The 'Merton School,'" *Archive for History of Exact Sciences* 8 (1971): 9–39; and "Medieval Concepts of the Latitude of Forms: The Oxford Calculators," *Archives d'histoire doctrinale et littéraire du moyen âge* 30 (1973): 223–83; and Murdoch, "From Social into Intellectual Factors," 289–98.

18. An especially good example is the treatment of the problem of the action of the will. It is analyzed—by Robert Holcot, Roger Rosetus, and others—in terms of its being a *continuous* action, thereby allowing the application of methods and conceptions developed and employed in analyzing continuous quantities in general. See the references in Murdoch, "From Social into Intellectual Factors," pp. 325–27, especially nn. 97, 100, 101.

19. One can naturally cite works with a specifically axiomatic format, such as Thomas Bradwardine's *Tractatus de continuo* and *De causa Dei* (see *Dictionary of Scientific Biography*, 2: 390–97), but I have in mind much more the careful elucidation of assumptions and conclusions within the *determinationes* of issues approached in standard scholastic *quaestio* form. The Aristotelian *quaestiones* of Jean Buridan and his followers are notable in this regard.

20. St. Bonaventure, *Comm. Sent.* lib. 2, dist. 1, p. 1, art. 1, quaest. 2 (*Opera omnia*, 2 [Quaracchi, 1885], 19–25). Bonaventure gives six "rationes ex propositionibus per se notis secundum rationem et philosophiam" purporting to establish the impossibility of an eternal world; all but one have to do with the infinite: "impossibile est infinito addi, . . . impossibile est infinita ordinari, . . . impossibile est infinita pertransiri, . . . impossibile est infinita a virtute finita comprehendi, . . . impossibile est infinita simul esse."

21. Perhaps the most outstanding instance of such a procedure occurs in the second decade of the fourteenth century when Henry of Harclay devotes two *quaestiones* to the possible (past and future) eternity of the world: *Utrum mundus potuit fuisse ab eterno* (MSS Vaticana, Burgh. lat. 171, 22v–24v; Assisi, Bibl. comm., 172, fols. 149r–152r); *Utrum mundus poterit durare in eternum a parte post* (see the manuscript references and remarks in Murdoch and Synan, "Two Questions on the Continuum"). The latter treats the problems of infinity and continuity per se with only a nod in the direction of the world's eternity, but even the former explicitly puts the infinite at the very center of the issue at stake.

22. Duns Scotus was the prime mover in bringing the continuum to center stage in discussing the problem of angelic motion; see J. E. Murdoch, "Naissance et développement de l'atomisme au bas moyen âge latin," *Cahiers d'études médiévales*, 2, *La science de la nature: théories et pratiques* (Montreal/Paris, 1974), pp. 28–30. The significance of relations for the Trinity is appreciated in almost all commentaries on the *Sentences*, but at times this reaches rather impressive proportions. Thus, Franciscus de Mayronis gives a veritable disquisition on *relationes* in his *Conflatus in Sent.* 1, dist. 29, quaest. 1–9 (ed. Venice, 1520), fols. 88r–93r.

23. *Impulsus* and *inclinationes* are central, for example, in Peter John Olivi's question *Utrum motus localis dicat aliquid absolutum supra mobile ipsum quod movetur localiter*; see Anneliese Maier, *Zwischen Philosophie und Mechanik*, in *Studien zur Naturphilosophie der Spätscholastik*, 5, [Rome, 1958], chap. 6. Taking a lead from Richard of Middleton (whom he is opposing), William of Alnwick makes *continuitas* the focal point of his investigation *Utrum motus sit de genere termini ad quem est* in his *Determinationes* quaest. 19 (MS Vat. Pal. lat. 1805, fol . 148r–151r); cf. Maier, *Zwischen Philosophie und Mechanik*, pp. 89–96.

24. See the references in Murdoch, "Naissance et développement," pp. 28–30, especially the *quaestio* of Walter Chatton there mentioned.

25. For example, the argument that (1) God could create an infinite magnitude (of stones, for instance) given an infinite past time by creating a stone on each past

day is transformed by claiming that (2) God could create an infinite magnitude by creating a finite amount in each of the infinity of proportional parts of a single hour. For (1) see, for example, Henry of Harclay (the first *quaestio* cited in note 21; MSS Vaticana, Burgh. lab. 171, fol. 23v; Assisi, Bibl. Comm. 172, fol. 150v): "tunc [scil., si mundus fuit eternus] posset esse continuum infinitum in actu, nam ab eterno potuisset Deus fecisse lapidem et ipsum coniunxisse alteri et esset nunc continuum infinitum." Cf. Peter John Olivi, *Quaestiones in II Sent.*, ed. B. Jansen (Quaracchi, 1922), 1:99. For (2) see Gregory of Rimini, *Super I Sent.* (ed. Venice, 1522; reprint ed., St. Bonaventure, N.Y., 1955), fol. 172r: "Nam data aliqua magnitudine cuba, potest Deus in cuiuslibet partis proportionalis unius hore instanti initiante cuilibet lateri illius magnitudinis addere equalem illi magnitudini cubam que unam per se magnitudinem constituant simul; ergo potest facere Deus magnitudinem undique infinitam; consequentia patet, quia in instanti terminante horam erit undique magnitudo infinita; et antecedens patet."

The problem of God's knowledge of the infinite derived from Augustine (*Civ. Dei* 12, chap. 18) and was discussed by any number of philosophers and theologians, especially Franciscans. See, for example, William of Alnwick, *Quaestiones disputatae de esse intelligibili et de quodlibet*, ed. A. Ledoux (Quaracchi, 1937), pp. 488–551.

26. Using the proportional parts of an hour becomes especially popular as a means to "generate" infinites. See Pierre Duhem, *Le système du monde*, 7 (Paris, 1956), chap. 1, passim.

27. To posit the existence of *res* beyond such would be, for Ockham, *frustra*. And that would run counter to his well-known "razor." On this topic see Jürgen Miethke, *Ockhams Weg zur Sozialphilosophie* (Berlin, 1969), pp. 238–44.

28. Compare (above, n. 16) Albertus Magnus's manner (ultimately deriving from Averroes *Phys.* 3, comm. 4) of putting the question of motion with that of Peter John Olivi (above, n. 23) and, especially, that of Ockham: *Comm. Sent.* 2, quaest. 9 (ed. Lyon, 1495; reprint ed., London, 1962): *Utrum motus sit vera res extra animam differens realiter a mobili et a termino*.

29. See M. A. Pernoud, "Innovation in William of Ockham's References to the 'Potentia Dei,'" *Antonianum* 45 (1970): 65–97.

30. One might, for example, treat natural and violent motion separately, or concentrate upon other properties of motion such as its acquisition of space or its intensibility or remissibility, in order to discover what kind of an entity it is. This kind of procedure is to an appreciable extent followed by John Dumbleton (above, n. 17) and, to a lesser degree, by Peter John Olivi (above, n. 23).

31. This is, at bottom, what is involved in Walter Chatton, *Comm. Sent.* 2, dist. 2, quaest. 2: *Utrum motus sit aliqua res positiva distincta ab absolutis rebus permanentibus* (MSS Florence, Bibl. naz., conv. soppr. C. 5. 357, fols. 185v–186v; Paris, Bibl. nat., lat. 15887, fols. 90r–91v), a *quaestio* that is directed precisely against Ockham's view of the matter.

32. See William of Ockham, *Philosophical Writings*, ed. and trans. P. Boehner (Edinburgh, 1957), pp. 2–16.

33. One might add that for Ockham *scientia* deals with *passiones* (not accidents) as predicated of *subiecta*, and they cannot be denied of any thing of which they are predicable. See T. K. Scott, "Ockham on Evidence, Necessity, and Intuition," *Journal of the History of Philosophy* 7 (1969): 27–49.

34. Thus, relative to the required continuity of motion, Ockham claims:

Continuitas motus non est alia res a rebus permanentibus, sed ex hoc dicitur motus continuus, quia semper res mobilis acquirit vel deperdit aliquid sine quiete sub aliquo praecise, ita videlicet, quod nulla talis propositio: hoc est sub hoc, vel hoc est in hoc et non in alio, possit verificari cum quibuscumque partibus contradictionis successive verificatis. Hoc enim est quiescere in aliquo, quando scilicet ista propositio copulativa: hoc est in hoc loco et non in alio, vel saltem ista: hoc est in hoc loco, potest verificari cum quibuscumque contradictionis successive verificatis. Ad continuitatem igitur motus sufficit, quod mobile in aliquo non quiescit vel sub aliquo praecise; sed quandocumque contingit verum dicere, quod mobile est sub hoc vel in hoc praecise, ita quod non contingit postea dicere, quod mobile est in hoc vel sub hoc praecise, tunc est motus. Quod potest fieri sine omni re distincta a rebus permanentibus per hoc solum, quod una res succedit alteri, vel per hoc, quod una et eadem res numero est primo in uno loco et postea sine quiete media in alio. [*De successivis* (Boehner), 62–63];

cf. Ockham's *Comm. Sent.* 2, quaest. 9 (Lyon), ad sig. mg. 1. Ockham treats the velocity of motion in a similar fashion (quaest. 9, ad sig. mg. o).

35. This way of labeling such an approach derives from the fact that the analysis in question used such terms as "noun," "verb," "proposition," "term," etc., which for the medieval were terms of "second intention" since they stood for elements of a language and not, like terms of "first intention" (e.g., "dog," "philosopher," etc.), for extramental, individual entities. On the whole distinction, see Ockham *Philosophical Writings* (Boehner, 56–58).

36. See, for example, the use of *suppositio* in St. Bonaventure, *Comm. Sent.* 1, dist. 4, art. unicus, quaest. 4.

37. Johannes Canonicus *Questiones in Phys.* 6, quaestio unica (MSS Florence, Bibl. naz., conv. soppr. C. 8. 22, fol. 119v; Vatic. lat. 3013, fol. 73r):

Et pro quibusdam aliis rationibus solvendis: Pro una. scilicet quod in continuo sunt plures partes quam infinite, quia quelibet pars est divisibilis in infinitum, applico istam regulam: Quod quandocunque arguitur ab alico termino communi supponente confuse tantum respectu alicuius magnitudinis ad eundem terminum supponentem personaliter respectu alicuius multitudinis, non est bona consequentia, quia sequitur fallacia figure dictionis. Quod declaratur in quadam consimili ratione. Solet enim probari a quibusdam quod multitudo non possit crescere in infinitum, quia, si sic, tunc ultra omnem multitudinem finitam datam esset dare multitudinem finitam maiorem; sed multitudo maior omni multitudine finita est multitudo infinita; ergo, si ultra omnem multitudinem finitam datam esset dare multitudinem finitam maiorem, sequeretur quod alica multitudo finita esset infinita, quod est impossibile. Quod autem ultra omnem multitudinem finitam datam esset dare multitudinem finitam maiorem, si multitudo posset crescere in infinitum, patet, quia quelibet singularis huius universalis foret vera, nam ultra hanc multitudinem finitam datam esset dare multitudinem finitam maiorem, et ultra illam et sic in infinitum. Ad istam rationem respondetur quod hic est fallacia figure dictionis, quoniam in maiori iste terminus "multitudo" in predicato prime propositionis supponit confuse tantum et dicit quale quid; in minori autem supponit tantum determinate respectu eiusdem multitudinis importate per signum universale; et ideo commutatur quale quid in hoc aliquid. Ita recte possunt solvi multe rationes iuxta istam materiam. Applicate, si vis.

For a similar instance in William of Alnwick see J. E. Murdoch, "*Mathesis in philosophiam scholasticam introducta*: The Rise and Development of the Application of Mathematics in Fourteenth Century Philosophy and Theology," in *Arts libéraux et philosophie au moyen âge, Actes du quatrième Congrès international de philosophie médiévale* (Montreal/Paris, 1969), p. 220.

38. Walter Burleigh *De puritate artis logicae Tractatus longior* ed. P. Boehner (St. Bonaventure, N.Y., 1955), p. 33: "Ex praedictis [scil. aliqua de suppositione] solvuntur difficultates, quae contingunt in scientia naturali et in aliis scientiis ex ignorantia praedictorum."

39. Robert Holcot *In Sent 2*, quaest 2: *Utrum Deus ab eterno sciverit se producturum mundum* (ed. Lyon, 1508, no foliation). Among the "other issues" this propositional analysis makes it easier for Holcot to raise are: *An re non existente, sint tales proposi-*

John E. Murdoch

tiones concedende: "Rosa intelligitur," "Rosa concipitur" et huiusmodi; An veritas propositionis sit alia res a propositione; and three subquestions dealing directly with the much-debated problem of the truth and knowledge of future contingent propositions.

40. Fritz Hoffmann, *Die theologische Methode des Oxforder Dominikanerlehrers Robert Holcot,* Beiträge zur Geschichte der Philosophie und Theologie des Mittelalters, Neue Folge 5 (Münster, 1971), pp. 153–57.

41. For example, William of Ockham *Comm. Sent.* 2, quaest. 8 (Lyon), ad sig. mg. M: "Si dicas quod hec est vera: omne quod est quando est necesse est, respondeo quod illud non est logice dictum, quia non est plus propositio necessaria necessitate conditionata quam necessitate cathegorica, quia omnis propositio est necessaria que est necessaria absolute; sed recte intelligentes intelligunt sic quod illa propositio est necessaria que est conditionata vel temporalis, alia est necessaria que est simpliciter cathegorica et non conditionalis nec temporalis."

42. Such application is found, for instance, throughout William Heytesbury's analysis of the sophism *Omne animal fuit in archa Noe; Sophismata* 24 (ed. Venice, 1494), 141v–142v.

43. *Comm. Sent.* 2, quaest. 9 (Lyon), ad sig. mg. H: "patet quia motus componitur ex affirmationibus, puta ex partibus acquisitis per motum, et negationibus aliarum partium sequentium que infinita sunt."

44. *Ibid.*: "Quod autem ad motum requiritur negatio patet, quia motus necessario includit successionem."

45. William of Ockham *De successivis* (Boehner), 46: "Et per tales negativas nulla alia res ponitur praeter res permanentes. Et per consequens tota ratio motus sine quacumque alia re potest salvari per hoc, quod corpus est in distinctis locis successive, et non quiescit in aliquo." It is interesting to note that Ockham finds support in Aristotle himself for his view of motion as "constituted of affirmations and negations" (*Comm. Sent.* 2, quaest. 9): "Ista est intentio Philosophi tertio *Physicorum* ubi dicit quod motus est actus entis in potentia secundum quod est in potentia; per hoc quod dicit quod est actus innuit hoc quod est positivum in motu quod acquiritur ipsi mobili, et per hoc quod dicit quod est in potentia et cetera, innuit negationem partis sequentis sine tamen corruptione partis prime vel deperditione aliqua, sicut quando aer illuminat recepit lumen sine deperditione alicuius positivi."

46. The *De successivis*, although not written by Ockham himself, is authentic in the sense that it is made up of quotes from his undoubtedly genuine (as yet unedited) *Expositio super libros physicorum*.

47. "Et isto modo alias dixi, quod motus componitur ex negationibus et affirmationibus." *De successivis* (Boehner), 47.

48. Ockham's major error is, of course, to fail to give some account of the relation of "occupation" a mobile successively has to different places.

49. An instructive example is Ockham's answer to the questions *Quid est mutatio?* or *Quid est quando aliquid mutatur?* (*De successivis* [Boehner, 40]:

Si autem quaeritur: Quid est mutatio?, quaerendo quid nominis, quia aliud quid non habet, potest responderi non per *aliquod nomen absolutum,* quod non est *connotativum* vel *respectivum,* sed per *nomen verbale,* quale est hoc nomen mutatio. Sicut si quaeratur: Quid est quando aliquid mutatur?, non debet responderi per *aliquod nomen absolutum* dicendo, quod est res, substantia vel qualitas, sicut si sic quaeram: Quid est mutatio?, non debet responderi, quod est res vel substantia vel qualitas. Sed ad istam quaestionem: Quid est quando aliquid mutatur?, debet responderi: quando aliquid mutatur, acquirit aliquid, quod prius non habuit, vel deperdit aliquid, quod prius habuit. Sic ad istam quaestionem: Quid est mutatio?, debet responderi per *nomen verbale* sic: mutatio est acquisitio alicuius vel deperditio alicuius; quae aequivalet isti: quando aliquid mutatur, acquirit vel deperdit aliquid.

Similar procedure is found throughout the *De successivis*.

[74]

50. *De successivis* (Boehner), 46–47:

Talis fictio nominum abstractorum ab adverbiis, conjunctionibus, praepositionibus, verbis, syncategorematibus facit multas difficultates, et multos ducit in errores. Imaginantur enim multi per hoc, quod sicut sunt nomina distincta, ita sint res distinctae correspondentes, ut tanta videlicet sit distinctio inter res significatas quanta est inter nomina significantia. Quod tamen non est verum. Sed aliquando eaedem res sunt significatae, et tamen est diversitas in modo logicali vel grammaticali significandi. Et ideo non-simultas non est aliqua alia res a rebus, quae possunt simul esse, sed significat, quod res non sunt simul. Et ideo in modernis temporibus propter errores subortos ex usu talium abstractorum melius esset in Philosophia propter simplices non uti talibus abstractis, sed tantum verbis, adverbiis, conjunctionibus, praepositionibus, syncategorematibus, sicut primario fuerunt instituta, quam fingere talia abstracta et uti eis. Immo si non esset usus talium abstractorum: motus, mutatio, mutabilitas, simultas, successio, quies et huiusmodi, parva esset respective difficultas de motu, mutatione, tempore et instanti et huiusmodi.

51. Scotus's argument, put in syllogistic form, is: "Eminentissimo impossibile est esse aliquid perfectius, sed nullo finito est impossibile aliquid esse perfectius; ergo eminentissimum est infinitum." Ockham's matching syllogism is: "Omnem sedentem impossibile est ambulare, nullum sanum pedibus est impossibile ambulare; ergo nullum sanum pedibus est sedens." On all of this see M. Tweedale, "Scotus and Ockham on the Infinity of the Most Eminent Being," *Franciscan Studies* 17 (1963): 257–67.

52. *Expositio in libros physicorum* (MS Oxford, Merton 293, fol. 69r); the context is that of the "potential existence" of the infinite (Ockham is commenting on *Phys.* 3, t. 57 = Bekker 206a18–29) and this is explained in terms of the infinite divisibility of some continuum and the successiveness that this divisibility necessarily possesses:

Quando esse predicatur de alico importante successionem, requiruntur multe propositiones tanquam exponentes quarum aliqua erit de preterito, aliqua de presenti, aliqua de futuro et aliqua negativa; et sub tali sensu conceduntur tales propositiones: 'divisio linee est infinita', 'linea potest dividi in infinitum,' que equivalent talibus: 'linea est divisa' vel 'potest dividi et post cuiuscumque partis divisionem potest alia pars dividi.' Sed contra hoc videtur quod Philosophus non loquitur hic de propositionibus [sed de re *add.* MS Bruges 557, 161r] dicens quod res potest dividi in infinitum; dicendum quod frequenter Philosophus ponit actus signatos loco actuum exercitorum et econverso; et non minus est realis, quia actus signatus et actus exercitus sibi correspondens convertuntur, et ideo non inconvenienter ponit unum loco alterius. Et ideo quando dicit Philosophus quod multipliciter est esse et quod aliquid est in actu et aliquid in potentia et huiusmodi, intendit actus signatos quibus correspondent actus exerciti. Causa autem quare aliquando ponit actus signatos pro actibus exercitis est brevitas sermonis, et eadem est causa quare loco propositionum exponentium ponitur una sola cuius sunt ille exponentes.

Compare Ockham's appeal for "support" from Aristotle as cited in n. 45 above.

53. Prime cases would be Jean Buridan and Gregory of Rimini.

54. Chatton, *Comm. Sent.* 2, dist. 2, quaest. 2 (MSS Florence, Bibl. naz., conv. soppr. C. 5. 357, fol. 185v; Paris, Bibl. nat., lat. 15887, fol. 90v):

Respondeo ergo aliter pro modo quod motus est aliqua res positiva preter res absolutas permanentes, respectus scilicet motionis passive mobilis ad motorem. Quia ubi propositio verificatur pro rebus simul existentibus, si cum rebus existentibus simul positis potest esse falsa, oportet ponere aliam. Sed hec est huiusmodi: "hoc movetur ab hoc agente," et ad veritatem huius non sufficiunt omnes res absolute possibiles nec negationes quomodocumque combinate absolutorum, quia omnibus eque presentibus posset moveri a Deo et tunc esset hec falsa. Ergo alia res requiritur, scilicet motio passiva.

John E. Murdoch

55. Most notably, I feel, in Peter John Olivi, *In Sent II* (Jansen), 36–39; the context is that of arguments proving Olivi's contention that God cannot create an actual infinite:

Secundum rationes enim mathematicas occurrit primo una generalis contradictio: aequale scilicet et non aequale; eadem enim erunt aequalia et non aequalia. . . . Forte dicetur ad praedicta . . . quod praedictae contradictiones non habent locum in infinitis materialiter et in particulari sumptis et quae secundum unam viam sunt finita, secundum alteram infinita: nec habent locum in infinitis respectu suarum partium indeterminatarum, sed solum respectu determinatarum. Dicetur enim quod licet altera partium infiniti sit infinita, non tamen propter hoc sequitur quod sit aequalis suo toti per respectum ad illum terminum secundum quem tam ipsa quam suum totum sunt finita, sed solum secundum illam viam secundum quam utrumque est infinitum.

56. The most impressive treatment is that of Henry of Harclay, who goes on at great length to explain how the axiom *Omne totum est maius sua parte* can be made to "fit with" infinites. See J. E. Murdoch, "The 'Equality' of Infinites in the Middle Ages," *Actes du XIe Congrès International d'Histoire des Sciences* (Warsaw/Cracow, 1968), 3:171–74.

57. The accomplishment was that of Gregory of Rimini. See Murdoch, "'Equality' of Infinites."

58. See V. P. Zoubov, "Traktat Bradvardina 'O Kontinuume,'" *Istoriko-matematicheskie Issledovaniia* 13 (1960): 385–440 (Latin text of the enunciations of the definitions, suppositions, and conclusions). The complete text of the *Tractatus* is in J. E. Murdoch, "Geometry and the Continuum in the Fourteenth Century: A Philosophical Analysis of Thomas Bradwardine's *Tractatus de continuo*," Ph.D. dissertation, University of Wisconsin, 1957.

59. Thomas Bradwardine, *Tractatus de continuo* (MS Torun, R 4° 2), p. 188:

Posset autem circa predicta fieri una falsigraphia: Avroys in commento suo super Physicorum (III, c. 31), ubi dicit, quod naturalis demonstrat continuum esse divisibile in infinitum et geometer hoc non probat, sed supponit tamquam demonstratum in scientia naturali, potest igitur impugnare demonstrationes geometricas prius factas dicendo: Geometriam ubique supponere continuum ex indivisibilibus non componi et illud demonstrari non posse. Sed illud non valet, quia suppositum falsum. Non enim ponitur inter demonstrationes geometricas continuum non componi ex indivisibilibus nec dyalecticer indiget⟨ur⟩ ubique, quoniam ⟨non⟩ in 5ᵗᵒ Elementorum Euclidis. Et similiter, nec geometer in aliqua demonstratione supponit continuum non componi ex infinitis indivisibilibus mediatis, quia, dato eius opposito, quelibet demonstratio non minus procedit, ut patet inductive scienti conclusiones geometricas demonstrare.

60. Further evidence of Bradwardine's awareness of the "logic of assumptions" is found in the comment made (by his *reportator* perhaps) to one of the *suppositiones* (*Omnes scientias veras esse ubi non supponitur continuum ex indivisibilibus componi*) he placed at the beginning of his *Tractatus* (MS Torun, R 4° 2, p. 156, and MS Erfurt, Ampl. 4° 385, fol. 18r): "Hoc dicit quia aliquando utitur declaratis in aliis scientiis quasi manifestis, quia nimis longum esset hec omnia declarare. Ubi autem tractant de compositione continui ex indivisibilibus non supponit eas veras esse propter petitionem principii evitandam."

An intriguing remark concerning the "independence" of the axioms of geometry relative to the eternity of the world is made by Boethius of Dacia (*Tractatus de aeternitate mundi*, ed. G. Sajó [Berlin, 1964], p. 49), but its full implications are not realized:

Hoc enim non sequitur ex principiis geometriae, quia oppositum consequentis potest stare cum antecedente, scilicet primum motum et mundum esse aeternum potest stare cum principiis geometriae et omnibus suis conclusionibus. Dato enim hoc falso quod motus primus et mundus sit aeternus, numquid propter hoc erunt principia geometriae falsa, ut a puncto ad punctum rectam lineam ducere, vel etiam punctus est, cuius pars non est, et cetera talia, vel etiam suae conclusiones? Constat quod non. Numquid omnes passiones [possibiles] in magnitudine eodem modo essent demonstrabiles de suis substantiis et per easdem causas, etiam si mundus esset aeternus, sicut et si mundus sit novus? Constat quod sic.

61. Some indication of the interest in this logic as exhibited in the medieval Euclid can be found in J. E. Murdoch, "The Medieval Euclid: Salient Aspects of the Translations of the *Elements* by Adelard of Bath and Campanus of Novara," *Revue de Synthèse* 89 (1968): 67–94.

62. Apart from the frequent pejorative use of the term *sophisma* to designate a piece of sophistical reasoning, it was used to cover the very specialized kind of logical literature that will be of interest to us here, but also was employed in what appear to be in many instances not much more than ordinary *quaestiones*, the major difference being that the traditional opening *utrum* is omitted and the *quaestio* is specifically called a *sophisma*. For an example of this kind of sophism, see Tetsuo Yokoyama, "Simon of Faversham's Sophisma: 'Universale est intentio,'" *Mediaeval Studies* 31 (1969): 1–14. This ambiguity in the use of the term renders it very difficult to make conclusions about the exact meaning of university regulations speaking of "disputationes de sophismatibus"; cf. J. A. Weisheipl, "Curriculum of the Faculty of Arts at Oxford in the Early Fourteenth Century," *Mediaeval Studies* 26 (1964): 154–56, 177–81. The standard introductory work on sophisms is still Martin Grabmann, *Die Sophismataliteratur des 12. und 13. Jahrhunderts mit Textausgabe eines Sophisma des Boetius von Dacien*, Beiträge zur Geschichte der Philosophie und Theologie des Mittelalters, 36.1 (Münster, 1940).

63. These sample sophismata can be found in any number of medieval treatises, but they are all, in effect, present in Albert of Saxony's collection of more than 250 sophisms: *Sophismata nuper emendata* (ed. Paris, 1495). The frequent appearance of the term *asinus* in these examples has some significance. In the later fourteenth century there arose collections of sophisms that so concentrated on this term that they were called *Sophismata asinina*; an example is Padua Univ. MS 1123, fols. 18r–22v, which contains 37 different resolutions of the sophism *Tu es asinus*. Note should also be made of the fact that I have purposely excluded *insolubilia* from this list of examples even though they too were considered (a subclass of) sophismata by some. *Insolubilia* in almost all instances present genuine logical or linguistic paradoxes and are not our concern here.

64. See William of Sherwood, *Treatise on Syncategorematic Terms*, pp. 28–29, 31–36. Unlike William, Peter of Spain appears to employ sophisms in his *Tractatus* not to illustrate already-given rules or distinctions, but rather to introduce additional problems or issues concerning specific syncategorematic terms.

65. Two anonymous thirteenth-century collections appear in MS Vat. lat. 7678, fols. 1r–72v, containing 76 sophismata; and MS Paris, BN lat. 16135, fols. 3r–103v, containing 38. See Grabmann, *Die Sophismataliteratur*, pp. 33–41, 50–51, although his lists must be corrected and supplemented from the manuscripts. Collections of sophismata, anonymous and otherwise, increase rapidly in the fourteenth century. Perhaps the most important and well-known are those of William Heytesbury (ed. Venice, 1494), Richard Killington (see n. 10 above), Albert of Saxony (*Sophismata nuper emendata*), and Jean Buridan (ed. Paris, 1500; English translation by T. K. Scott, New York, 1966). There are more *physicalia* in the collections of Heytesbury and Killington. Indeed, Heytesbury's *sophismata* were edited together with his *Regule solvendi sophismata*, for the most part a work in natural philosophy using sophismata as an analytic tool.

66. Thus, the technique or rule one was being urged to become as expert as

possible in employing might be (for logic): "An inference from a term placed after an affirmative distribution to the same term placed before the affirmative distribution does not hold" and one of the sophisms relevant to it, "Every man is one man alone" (William of Sherwood, *Treatise on Syncategorematic Terms*, p. 31); or (in natural philosophy) the rule might be:
"The speed of the intension and remission of motion is measured in terms of the acquisition or loss of the latitude of motion involved and not in terms of the proportion of the degrees of this very same latitude lost or acquired" and the sophism (in slightly simplified form): "If a motion A begins to undergo uniform intension from degree C until it reaches a degree double C while a motion B during the same time is uniformly remitted from the same degree C to rest, then it can be argued that A is not intended with a swiftness equal to that of the remission of motion B" (William of Heytesbury, *Regule solvendi sophismata*, [ed. Venice, 1494], fols. 41v–42v).

67. See Murdoch, "From Social into Intellectual Factors," pp. 303–7.

68. Cf. J. E. Murdoch, "A Central Method of Analysis in Fourteenth-Century Science," *XIVth International Congress of the History of Science, Proceedings No. 2* (Tokyo, 1975), pp. 68–71. Note should also be taken of the fact that the kind of sophismata of which we have been speaking became so ingrained at Oxford that they are found populating numerous codices of Wycliffite logic and natural philosophy. Various other aspects of English sophisms are discussed by Neal W. Gilbert, "Richard de Bury and the 'Quires of Yesterday's Sophisms,'" in *Philosophy and Humanism, Renaissance Essays in Honor of Paul Oskar Kristeller*, ed. Edward P. Mahoney (New York, 1976), pp. 229–57.

69. Cf. nn. 45 and 52 above.

70. For Swineshead, see the article by Murdoch and Sylla in *Dictionary of Scientific Biography*, 13:184–213. John Dumbleton also shows some hesitation in deciding between the rival views he is examining of the nature of motion: "Licet hec positio tertia videatur falsum pro parte, continere potest tamen pro parte fundari" (MS Cambridge, Peterhouse 272, fol. 30v).

71. Thus, in examining the position that motion is an accident existing in the mobile, Dumbleton creates additional objections to it by considering the allowable infinity of local motion and the requisite forces and resistances operative in local motion: "Sed cum motus [localis] potest intendi in infinitum intensive, ergo motus non est res distincta de novo producta in motum. . . . Item omnis motus localis in inferioribus motis fit cum resistentia et iuxta proportionem quam habet motor ad medium resistens; sed cum actio motoris est in medium resistens et non in se nec in materiam primam, ergo motus localis in aere esset accidens in aere sive in alio medio resistente et non in ipso moto" (MSS Cambridge, Peterhouse 272, fol. 30r, and London, BM Royal 10. B. XIV, fol. 64v).

Something of the contrary of Dumbleton's multiplication of objections can be seen in Richard Swineshead's opusculum *In librum de caelo* (MSS Cambridge, Gonville & Caius 499/268, fol. 204r–211r; Worcester Cath. F. 35, fol. 65v–69v). This brief work begins by an examination of Aristotle's arguments against the possible circular motion of an infinite line (*De caelo* 1, t. 35 = 271b23 ff.) and in the course of treating this issue Swineshead establishes a number of "lemmas" establishing the relations between the vertex angles of isosceles triangles with certain given bases, but then never seems to get around to applying these results to the problem at hand. Is this yet another example of the "critical" character of fourteenth-century philosophy?

72. Thus, Henry of Harclay, Walter Chatton, and Gerard of Odo adopt an atomist or indivisibilist position concerning the composition of continua not because of any major positive functions that atomism can serve, but rather apparently because they perceive a certain inadequacy in Aristotle's contrary position. Cf. Murdoch, "Naissance et développement," pp. 28–30.

73. Thus the anonymous commentator on the *Sentences* in MS Vat. lat. 986 brings

up rules of measure presumably to be applied in measuring the scale of the perfections of species but then has to admit that they are inappropriate for this task. Or Pierre Ceffons invents an elaborate mathematics of the "infinitesimal" (horn angles, to be specific) in order to explain the problems of mutual excess and incomparability between radically diverse species, but then appears to deny the applicability of his creation. On both of these examples see Murdoch, "*Mathesis*," pp. 240–46.

74. The author is again Pierre Ceffons; see Murdoch, "*Mathesis*," nn. 57 and 111.

75. Eugenio Garin, "La cultura fiorentina nella seconda metà del Trecento e i 'barbari Britanni,'" in his *L'età nuova. Richerche di storia della cultura dal XII al XVI secolo* (Naples, 1969), pp. 139–77.

76. Robert Spindler, ed., *The Court of Sapience* (Leipzig, 1927), ll. 1849–55, 1866–69.

77. It is extremely likely that our anonymous poet drew his knowledge of these "elements" from a Wycliffite source. Not only is the timing right, but logical and philosophical writings by Wycliffe's followers furnish exactly what the poem exhibits. Thus a manuscript like Oxford, New College 289, contains numerous sophisms plus the Wycliffite William Mylverley's *De differt* (fols. 86r–94r), *De scire* (fols. 95r–102v), and *De incipit* (fols. 75v–86r). MS Oxford, Corpus Christi College 116 contains similar, indeed much of the same, material. For *Tu es asinus*, see n. 63.

V

"But We Are Spirits of Another Sort": The Dark Side of Love and Magic in A Midsummer Night's Dream

David Bevington
University of Chicago

When Oberon instructs Puck, in act 3, scene 2 of *A Midsummer Night's Dream*, to overcast the night with "drooping fog as black as Acheron," and to lead the "testy rivals" Demetrius and Lysander astray so that they will not actually harm one another in their rivalry, while Oberon for his part undertakes to obtain the changeling boy from Titania whom he will then release from her infatuated love of Bottom, Puck replies that the two of them will have to work fast. Such fairy doings need to be accomplished by night, insists Puck. With the approaching break of day, and the shining of Aurora's harbinger or morning star, ghosts and damned spirits will have to trip home to churchyards and their "wormy beds" beneath the ground. Puck's implication seems clear: he and Oberon, being spirits of the dark, are bound by its rules to avoid the light of day.

Just as clearly, however, Oberon protests that Puck is wrong in making such an assumption. "But we are spirits of another sort," Oberon insists.

> I with the Morning's love have oft made sport,
> And, like a forester, the groves may tread
> Even till the eastern gate, all fiery red,
> Opening on Neptune, with fair blessèd beams
> Turns into yellow gold his salt green streams.
>
> [3.2. 388–93][1]

Oberon may frolic until late in the dawn, though by implication even he may not stay abroad all day. The association of Oberon with sunlight and dawn is thus more symbolic than practical; it disassociates him from spirits of the dark, even though he must finish up this night's work before night is entirely past. He concedes to Puck the need for hurry: "But notwithstanding, haste; make no delay. / We may effect this business yet ere day." The concession implies that Oberon has made his point about sporting with the dawn not to refute Puck's call for swiftness, but to refute Puck's association of the fairies with ghosts and damned spirits.[2]

This debate between Oberon and Puck reflects a fundamental tension in the play between comic reassurance and the suggestion of something dark and threatening. Although the fairies act benignly, Puck continually hints at a good deal more than simple mischief. The forest itself is potentially a place of violent death and rape, even if the lovers experience nothing more than fatigue, anxiety, and being torn by briars. In the forest, moreover, the experience of love invites all lovers to consider, however briefly, the opportunity for sexual reveling freed from the restraints of social custom. Of late, Jan Kott has shown to us most forcefully this dark side of love; indeed, he has done so too forcefully, and with an often exaggerated effect upon contemporary productions of this and other plays.[3] Still, his insight has something to commend it. If his overstated emphasis on the dark side of love can perhaps be seen as a manifestation of the new sexual freedom of the 1960s, the sometimes overheated reactions against Kott can perhaps be related to the reluctance of most of us to give up the romanticized and sentimentalized nineteenth-century reading of the play (epitomized in Mendelssohn's incidental music) to which Kott is addressing his attack. Even today, we find it distasteful to speak openly of sexual longing in this comedy, for fear of dealing grossly with the play's delicately understated portrayal of Eros. My purpose, however, is to suggest that in its proper context the dark side of love is seldom very far away in this play.

Let us return to the debate between Oberon and Puck, and to Shakespeare's dramatic purpose in presenting to us both the king of fairies and his mischievous attendant. This purpose is not restricted to the fairies' function in the plot, in which Puck comically misapplies Oberon's ambiguous instructions about the love juice or extemporaneously creates a monster with whom Titania is to fall in love. Puck constantly brings before our eyes a more threatening vision of fairydom than is apparent in Oberon's more regal pronouncements. In part, of course, he is the practical joker making Oberon laugh at his ability to mimic a filly foal, or a three-foot stool, or Demetrius and Lysander. Puck is infinitely versatile in changing shapes, just as he can also put a girdle round the earth in forty minutes. On the other hand, Puck also loves to frighten people. He gladly confesses to being the elf who "frights the maidens of the villagery" (2.1.35). It is he who conjures up, for the delectation of the audience, a morbid image of nighttime as fearful, and as associated with gaping graves in churchyards, ghosts and damned spirits, screeching owls, and howling wolves:

> Now the hungry lion roars,
> And the wolf behowls the moon;
> Whilst the heavy ploughman snores,
> All with weary task fordone.
> Now the wasted brands do glow,
> Whilst the screech owl, screeching loud,
> Puts the wretch that lies in woe
> In remembrance of a shroud.
> Now it is the time of night
> That the graves, all gaping wide,
> Every one lets forth his sprite,
> In the churchyard paths to glide.

> [5.1.360–71]

Although, as he says, the fairies are now "frolic," their usual custom is to run "By the triple Hecate's team / From the presence of the sun." Earlier, too, as we have seen, Puck associates his own nocturnal activities with "night's swift dragons" and with ghosts "wand'ring here and there," "damnèd spirits all, / That in crossways and floods have burial," hastening home to their "wormy beds" before the break of day, lest the daylight should "look their shames upon" (3.2.379–85).

Even in the action of the play, Puck does in fact frighten many of the persons he meets—virtually all of them, in fact, except Bottom. As he chases Quince, Snout, and the rest from their rehearsal spot in a forest clearing, he makes the incantation:

[82]

I'll follow ypu; I'll lead you about a round,
Through bog, through bush, through brake, through brier.
Sometime a horse I'll be, sometime a hound,
A hog, a headless bear, sometime a fire;
And neigh, and bark, and grunt, and roar, and burn,
Like horse, hound, hog, bear, fire, at every turn.

[3.1.96–101]

And he later reports to his master, with glee, the startling effect upon the rude mechanicals created by Bottom's reemergence from his hawthorne tiring house with an ass's head on his shoulders:

When they him spy,
As wild geese that the creeping fowler eye,
Or russet-pated choughs, many in sort,
Rising and cawing at the gun's report,
Sever themselves and madly sweep the sky;
So at his sight away his fellows fly,
And at our stamp here o'er and o'er one falls;
He murder cries and help from Athens calls.
Their sense thus weak, lost with their fears thus strong,
Made senseless things begin to do them wrong,
For briers and thorns at their apparel snatch:
Some, sleeves—some, hats; from yielders all things catch.

[3.2.19–30]

Our own laughter at this comic chase should not obscure the fact that Puck creates truly frightening illusions in the forest. Similarly, our sense of assurance that Demetrius and Lysander will come to no harm must not cause us to forget that Puck's game with them is to lead them astray, like those night-wanderers whom he is known to mislead, "laughing at their harm" (2.1.39).

In the relationship of Puck and Oberon, it is Puck who tends to stress the irrational and frightening while Oberon's position is that of a ruler insisting on the establishment of proper obedience to his authority.[4] When Puck mistakenly applies the love-juice intended for Demetrius to Lysander's eyes, thereby inducing Lysander to desert his true love for Helena, Oberon's first reaction is one of dismay:

What hast thou done? Thou hast mistaken quite
And laid the love-juice on some true-love's sight.
Of thy misprison must perforce ensue
Some true-love turned, and not a false turned true.

[3.2.88–91]

Whereupon the fairy king immediately orders Puck to find Helena and return with her, so that Demetrius (who now lies asleep at their feet) can be induced to love her. Oberon seeks always to right unhappy love. His insistence that he and his followers are fairies of "another sort" is thus an appropriate and consistent stance for him, even if what he says does not always square with Puck's role as the hobgoblin who skims milk of its cream, prevents milk from turning into butter, or deprives ale of its "barm" or head. Oberon's very presence at the wedding is intended to assure that such things won't happen to Theseus, Hippolyta, and the rest of the happy young people about to marry; Oberon guarantees that their issue "Ever shall be fortunate," free of "mole, harelip, nor scar," or any other "blots of Nature's hand" (5.1.395–400).[5]

Together, Oberon and Puck represent contrasting forces within the fairy kingdom. Perhaps their functions can best be reconciled by reflecting that their chief power to do good lies in withholding the mischief of which they are capable. Like Apollo in book 1 of the *Iliad*, whom the Greek warriors venerate as the god of health because he is also terrifyingly capable of sending plagues, Oberon is to be feared because he has the authority both to prevent birth defects and other marks "prodigious, such as are / Despisèd in nativity" (5.1.401–2), and to inflict them. Only when placated by men and called by such names as Hobgoblin or "sweet Puck" will these spirits work for men and bring them good luck.

The forest shares many of these same ambivalent qualities as do the fairies. It is in part a refuge for young lovers fleeing the sharp Athenian law, a convenient and secluded spot for clandestine play rehearsals, and a fragrant bower for the fairy queen decked out "With sweet musk-roses, and with eglantine" (2.1.252). For the young lovers, however, as their quest for amorous bliss grows more and more vexed, the forest becomes increasingly a place of darkness, estrangement, and potential violence. Demetrius warns Helena, in an attempt to be rid of her,

> You do impeach your modesty too much
> To leave the city and commit yourself
> Into the hands of one that loves you not,
> To trust the opportunity of night
> And the ill counsel on a desert place
> With the rich worth of your virginity.
>
> [2.1.214–19]

Demetrius recognizes the opportunity for a loveless rape and briefly recognizes his own potential for such sexual violence, though he is also virtuous enough to reject the temptation. The alternative he offers Helena is scarcely more kind: he will run from her and leave her "to the mercy of wild beasts" (l. 228).

The ever-present moon shares this same ambivalence. Although it is at times the beneficent moon shining at its full on the palace wood to facilitate a rehearsal (1.2) or through a casement window of the great chamber where the final performance of "Pyramus and Thisbe" is to take place (3.1), it is contrastingly an old waning moon, associated with age and inhibition of pleasures, lingering the desires of would-be lovers "Like to a stepdame or a dowager, / Long withering out a young man's revenue" (1.1.6–7). More ominously, the moon is "the governess of floods," who "Pale in her anger, washes all the air, / That rheumatic diseases do abound" (2.1.103–5), whenever the fairy king and queen are at enmity. Even if the "chaste beams of the wat'ry moon" call up associations of that "fair vestal," Queen Elizabeth (2.1.158–64), and seem to offer assurances of the kind of divine protection afforded the young lady in Milton's *Comus*, the moon is not permitted to shine continually throughout the nighttime misadventures of this play. Oberon orders Puck, as we have seen, to overcast the night. "The starry welkin cover thou anon / With drooping fog as black as Acheron" (3.2.355–57). In the ensuing darkness, the lovers stress repeatedly their sense of bewilderment and discouragement. "O weary night, O long and tedious night," complains Helena, "Abate thy hours" (3.2.431–32). The word "weary" sounds a choric note of repetition in Hermia's entrance, immediately following the speech just quoted: "Never so weary, never so in woe, / Bedabbled with the dew, and torn with briers, / I can no further crawl" (ll. 442–44). Lysander, having fallen as he says "in dark uneven way," has already given up pursuit of Demetrius, who all unawares joins his archrival "on this cold bed" (ll. 417, 429). Although the lovers are together, and although their tribulations are now at an end, the nighttime experience has been one of separation, humiliation, and defeat. As Puck observes earlier, they have been reduced to sleeping "On the dank and dirty ground" (2.2.75).

Nighttime in the forest repeatedly conveys the sense of estrangement and misunderstanding with which the lovers are afflicted. When Puck creates a pitchy darkness into which he can lead Lysander and Demetrius, he is not manufacturing mischief out of nothing but is giving expression to their rivalry in love. As a stage manager of his own little play, he allows the men to parody their own tendencies toward petty vengefulness. The fact that the two young men are rather much alike, that their contention can be resolved by a simple solution (since Demetrius did in fact pay court to Helena before the play began, and need only return to his original attachment to her), adds to the sense of comedy by heightening the comic discrepancy between their anger and its lack of objective cause. Puck's manipulation serves the benign effect of showing (to the lovers themselves, in retrospect) the ridiculousness of exaggerated contentiousness. In a similar way Puck uses night and darkness as an emblem to expose the catty jealousies of the two young women and their tendency toward morbid self-pity. The effect of such cleansing exposure is a comic purgation. Puck is a creature of the night, but he uses darkness to produce ultimate illumination. He mocks pretensions, even in himself, even in the play to which he belongs: "If we shadows have offended, / Think but this, and all is mended— / That you have but slumb'red here / While these visions did appear" (5.1.412–15).

Darkness and the forest, then, offer the lovers a glimpse of their inner selves. Often, this glimpse suggests much about human nature that is not merely perverse and jealous, but libidinous. Here again Jan Kott offers helpful insights, though he has surely gone too far. The motif on which the action of the play is based, that of escape into a forest on the eve of Mayday (Walpurgisnacht) or on

Midsummer's Eve, is traditionally erotic.[6] The four lovers are discovered the next morning asleep on the ground, in a compromising position certainly, though not in flagrante delicto. "Begin these woodbirds but to couple now?" asks Theseus humorously and continues to remain skeptical toward the lovers' story of their night —a skepticism prompted in part, one imagines, by their insistence that they have slept apart from one another. We know, in fact, that their night has been a continuous series of proposed matings without any actual consummations. "One turf shall serve as pillow for us both," Lysander suggests to Hermia as night comes on. "One heart, one bed, two bosoms, and one troth" (2.2.41–42). She finds his rhetoric pretty but insists on a propriety that is not mere primness. "Such separation as may well be said / Becomes a virtuous bachelor and a maid, / So far be distant," she instructs him (ll. 58–60). She wants her lover to move away just a little, but not too much. Hermia knows, because of the person she is, that freedom to escape the harsh Athenian law does not mean the license to try anything and that she can justify her elopement only by voluntary obedience to a code she holds to be absolutely good and that she never questions. The serpent of which she dreams, crawling on her breast to eat her heart away while Lysander watches smilingly (ll. 146–50), is not an image of her own licentiousness but of an infidelity in which she is the innocent victim. Demetrius too would never presume to take advantage of Helena's unprotected condition, however much he may perceive an opportunity for rape. Kott seriously distorts the context of the love imagery in this play when he discovers sodomistic overtones in Helena's likening herself to a spaniel;[7] her meaning, as she clearly explains, is that she is like a patient, fawning animal whose master responds to affection with blows and neglect.

Repeatedly in this play, a presumption of man's licentiousness is evoked, only to be answered by the conduct of the lovers themselves. This representation of desire almost but not quite satisfied is to be sure a titillating one, but it looks forward as do the lovers themselves to legitimate consummation in marriage and procreation. At the very end, the lovers do all go to bed while Oberon speaks of the issue that will surely spring from their virtuous coupling. Earlier, Theseus has proposed to await the marriage day for his consummation, even though he captured his wife through military force; why else should he complain of the aged moon that "lingers" his desires "Like to a stepdame or a dowager"? (Hippolyta, with a maiden's traditional reluctance, seems more content with the four-day delay than does her amorous bridegroom.) The tradesmen's play serves as one last comic barrier to the achievement of desire, although it is mercifully brief and can be performed without epilogue in the interest of further brevity. Such waiting only makes the moment of final surrender more pleasurable and meaningful.

The conflict between sexual desire and rational restraint is, then, an essential tension throughout the play reflected in the images of dark and light. This same tension exists in the nature of the fairies and of the forest. The ideal course seems to be a middle one, between the sharp Athenian law on the one hand with its threat of death or perpetual chastity, and a licentiousness on the other hand that the forest (and man's inner self) proposes with alacrity, but from which the lovers are saved chiefly by the steadfastness of the women. They, after all, remain constant; it is the men who change affections under the effect of Oberon's love potion. (In the fairy plot, to be sure, we find a reverse symmetry that is surely intentional: the woman is inconstant, since it is Titania, the fairy queen, who takes a new lover. With a similar reversal the obstacle to love in the fairy plot is internal, since the king and queen are divided by their own quarrel for mastery in love, whereas in the plot of the four lovers the original obstacle is the external one of parental opposition.)[8]

This tension between licentiousness and self-mastery is closely related also to the way in which the play itself constantly flirts with genuine disaster but controls that threat through comic reassurance. Hermia is threatened with death in act 1, or with something almost worse than death—perpetual maidenhood, and yet we know already from the emphasis on love and marriage that all such threats to happiness are ultimately to prove illusory. Lysander and Hermia speak of "War, death, or sickness" and of other external threats to love, but are resolved on a plan of escape that will avoid all these. Repeatedly in the forest the lovers fear catastrophe only to discover that their senses have been deceiving them. "But who is here?"

[88]

asks Helena as she comes across a sleeping man, Lysander, on the ground: "Dead, or asleep?" (2.2.100–101). When, shortly afterwards, Hermia awakes to find herself deserted, she sets off after her strangely absent lover: "Either death, or you, I'll find immediately" (l. 156). The choice seems dire, but the comic sense of discrepancy assures us that the need for such a choice is only a chimera. Later, again, when Helena concludes that all her erstwhile friends have turned against her for some inexplicable reason, she determines to leave them: "'Tis partly my own fault, / Which death or absence soon shall remedy" (3.2.243–44). Only in the story of Pyramus and Thisbe, with its hilarious presentation of the very tragedy of misunderstanding that did not occur in *A Midsummer Night's Dream*, does comic reassurance fail. Instead of Helena's "Dead, or asleep?" the order is reversed. "Asleep, my love?" asks Thisbe as she finds Pyramus on the ground. "What, dead, my dove?" (5.1.316–17).[9]

What, finally, of love and sex among the fairies? When we come to the sexual escapades of Oberon and Titania, especially the latter, we come to what is for Kott the central image of the dark side of love. Bottom's ass's head, insists Kott, is grossly animal, especially since "from antiquity up to the Renaissance the ass was credited with the strongest sexual potency and among all quadrupeds was supposed to have the longest and hardest phallus." Because Titania herself is presumably delicate and fair, the violent image of her coupling with Bottom calls to Kott's mind those "white Scandinavian girls I used to see on the *rue de la Harpe* or *rue de la Huchette*, walking and clinging tightly to Negroes with faces grey or so black that they were almost undistinguishable from the night."[10]

This reading has proved too strong for most critics and indeed it exaggerates distastefully and needlessly. I say needlessly because the coupling of Titania and Bottom has long been regarded as a comic version of Beauty and the Beast.[11] As in that fairy story, or as in Ovid's narratives of transformation in love, such pairing of opposites is plainly suggestive of the yoking of the ethereal and the carnal in human nature.

The fairies of *A Midsummer Night's Dream* do not govern themselves by the conventional sexual mores of the humans.[12] As we have already seen, many things are inverted in the mirror-image

[89]

world of fairydom: it is the woman rather than the man who is inconstant, the obstacles to love are internal rather than external,
and so on. Similarly, the quarrel of Oberon and Titania reflects the
recently completed struggle for mastery between Theseus and Hippolyta, and yet is conducted according to the peculiar customs of
the fairy kingdom. Titania's love for Theseus is apparently the
occasion of her current visit to Athens, in order that she may be at
Theseus's wedding; yet her love for the Athenian king has taken
strange forms. According to Oberon, Titania's love for Theseus
prompts her to "lead him through the glimmering night / From
Perigenia, whom he ravishèd, / And make him with fair Aegles
break his faith, / With Ariadne, and Antiopa" (2.1.77–80). Titania
to be sure denies the charge. The point is, however, that Oberon
considers his queen perfectly capable of expressing her love for
Theseus by encouraging him to ravish and then reject in turn a
series of human mistresses. This is the sort of mysterious affection
that only a god could practice or understand. Oberon's behavior in
love is no less puzzling from a human vantage: he punishes Titania
for denying him the changeling boy by forcing her to take a gross
and foolish lover. These gods make a sport of inconstancy.

The rivalry about the changeling boy is equally bizarre if measured in human terms. Conceivably, as Kott suggests, Oberon desires the boy as his own minion, although (like so much of what
Kott claims) the boy's erotic status cannot be proved from a reading
of the text. We are told only that he is a "lovely boy" whom "jealous
Oberon" desires as a "Knight of his train" to be his "henchman"
(2.1.22–25, 121). When Oberon has succeeded in winning the boy
from her, he has the youth sent to his "bower in fairyland" (4.1.60).
This slender evidence seems deliberately ambiguous. Any attempts
to depict Oberon as bisexual surely miss the point that the fairies'
ideas concerning love are ultimately unknowable and incompre-
hensible. We mortals can laugh at our own libidinous tendencies
when we see them mirrored in the behavior of the immortals, but
we can never fathom how distant those immortals are from the
ordinary pangs of human affection. Oberon is not so busy teaching
Titania a lesson that he fails to enjoy Puck's "fond pageant" on the
theme of human passion: "Lord, what fools these mortals be."

Titania does of course undergo an experience of misdirected

love that is analogous to human inconstancy in love and that is prompted by the same love-juice applied to the eyes of Demetrius and Lysander. To confound her with a mortal is, however, to follow Kott's erroneous lead of imagining her as a white-skinned Scandinavian in Paris coupling with a dark-skinned man. That anachronistic image may well convey to us an aura of the exotic and bizarre, but in doing so it introduces a false note of sexual perversity and compulsion. Titania abundantly demonstrates that she is motivated by no such human drive. Her hours spent with Bottom are touchingly innocent and tender. Like the royal creature that she is, she forbids Bottom to leave her presence. Even if he is her slave, however, imprisoned in an animal form, she is no Circean enchantress teaching him enslavement to sensual appetite. Instead, her mission is to "purge thy mortal grossness so / That thou shalt like an airy spirit go" (3.1.145–46). It is because she is prompted by such ethereal considerations that she feeds him with apricots and dewberries, fans the moonbeams from his sleeping eyes, and the like. As Oberon reports later to Puck, having kept close watch over Titania, she graces the hairy temples of Bottom's ass's head "With coronet of fresh and fragrant flowers" (4.1.51). Rather than descending into the realm of human passion and perversity, she has attempted to raise Bottom into her own. Bottom, for his part, speaking the part of the wise fool, has noted the irrationality of love but has submitted himself to deliciously innocent pleasures that are, for him, mainly gastronomic. Titania, and Shakespeare too, have indeed purged his mortal grossness, not by making him any less funny, but by showing how the tensions in this play between the dark and the affirmative side of love are reconciled in the image of Titania and the ass's head.

NOTES

1. Quotations are from *A Midsummer Night's Dream*, The Pelican Shakespeare, edited by Madeleine Doran (Baltimore, 1959). My title for this essay somewhat resembles that of Marjorie B. Garber in her chapter, "Spirits of Another Sort," from *Dream in Shakespeare* (New Haven, 1974), but our critical purposes are essentially different.

2. Roger Lancelyn Green, "Shakespeare and the Fairies," *Folklore* 73 (1962): 89–103, stresses his belief that the fairies of this play are not evil or malicious, like many spirits of folklore. So does K. M. Briggs (*The Anatomy of Puck* [London, 1959]). M. W. Latham (*The Elizabethan Fairies* [New York, 1930]) contends also that the fairies in *A Midsummer Night's Dream* are unthreatening, though he concedes that Shakespeare demonstrates in other plays a power among the fairies for trouble-making. David Young (*Something of Great Constancy* [New Haven, 1966]), on the other hand, ably shows what is threatening about Puck; see, for example, p. 28. See also W. Moelwyn Merchant, "*A Midsummer Night's Dream*: a Visual Re-creation," in *Early Shakespeare*, ed. John Russell Brown and Bernard Harris, Stratford-upon-Avon Studies 3 (London, 1961), pp. 165–85; G. K. Hunter, *William Shakespeare: The Late Comedies* (London, 1962), p. 16; and Michael Taylor, "The Darker Purpose of *A Midsummer Night's Dream*," *Studies in English Literature* 9 (1969): 257–73.

3. Jan Kott, *Shakespeare Our Contemporary*, trans. Boloslaw Taborski (New York, 1964).

4. Howard Nemerov, "The Marriage of Theseus and Hippolyta," *Kenyon Review* 18 (1956): 633–41, contrasts the rationality of Oberon with the magical, fabulous, and dramatic character of Hippolyta.

5. On the relation of fairy magic to birth marks, see K. M. Briggs, *Pale Hecate's Team* (London, 1962).

6. On customs associated with Midsummer Night, see Sir James Frazer, *The Golden Bough*, abridged ed. (London, 1933), chap. 10, p. 133, quoted in Peter F. Fisher, "The Argument of *A Midsummer Night's Dream*," *Shakespeare Quarterly* 8 (1957): 307–10; also Lou Agnes Reynolds and Paul Sawyer, "Folk Medicine and the Four Fairies of *A Midsummer Night's Dream*," *Shakespeare Quarterly* 10 (1959): 513–21; and C. L. Barber, *Shakespeare's Festive Comedy* (Princeton, 1959). Ernest Schanzer ("The Central Theme of *A Midsummer Night's Dream*," *University of Toronto Quarterly* 20 [1951]: 233–38) observes that the central events of the play seem really to have taken place on the eve of May Day. Young (*Something of Great Constancy*, p. 24) discusses the associations of the action with both Midsummer Eve and May Day.

7. Kott, *Shakespeare Our Contemporary*, p. 225.

8. Young (*Something of Great Constancy*) discusses "mirroring" of this sort on pp. 95 ff.

9. On "Pyramus and Thisbe" as "a foil to the entire play of which it is a part," see R. W. Dent, "Imagination in *A Midsummer Night's Dream*," *Shakespeare Quarterly* 15 (1964): 115–29.

10. Kott, *Shakespeare Our Contemporary*, p. 227.

11. See, for example, Young, *Something of Great Constancy*, p. 15.

12. As Alfred Harbage observes in *As They Liked It* (New York, 1947), "For the most part we must look for our moral defect among quarrelsome fairies" (p. 140). To Harbage, the fairy scenes in *A Midsummer Night's Dream* are unique in Shakespeare in their lack of appeal to standards of moral conduct and to choice between right and wrong (p. 6). See also E. C. Pettet, *Shakespeare and the Romance Tradition* (London, 1949), p. 112, on the thematic relationship between the Oberon-Titania quarrel and that of the human lovers.

VI

The Habsburg World Empire and the Revival of Ghibellinism[1]

John M. Headley

The University of North Carolina at Chapel Hill

On 8 September 1517 Charles of Burgundy set sail from Flushing, Zeeland, in order to claim his Spanish kingdoms, recently left rulerless by the death of his grandfather, Ferdinand of Aragon.[1] As the fleet that bore the youthful king to Castile stood out toward the English Channel, there could be descried, painted on the sails of the royal flagship, the emblem devised by the court physician Marlianus: the two columns of Hercules and the intertwined inscription *Plus Oultre*—"still further." To the knights of the Order of the Golden Fleece who had gathered in the choir of Saint Gudule the previous year to hear Marlianus's oration, there could have been little doubt as to the emblem's preeminent meaning. For at that time the orator had set forth a worldwide empire and called Charles a new Hercules or Atlas superbly qualified to bear its responsibilities. Nor for that matter could there have been much doubt in the minds of the awed populace of Brussels, as it watched in March of the same year the funeral cortege of Ferdinand of Aragon wind its way through the narrow streets of the city. There stood in the last car, for all to behold, a soldier in full armor with sword upraised surrounded by Amerindians and at the back of the car a golden globe with the motto *Ulterius nisi morte*, suggestive of universal expansion. And in the young king himself there could be

*I wish to express my gratitude to the John Simon Guggenheim Memorial Foundation for a grant that allowed me to accomplish some of the research for this paper. I also want to take this opportunity to thank the staff of the Biblioteca Reale di Torino, the Bibliothèque municipale de Besançon, the Bibliothèque Royale Albert Ier, the Münchner Universitätsbibliothek, the Haus-Hof und Staatsarchiv, the Biblioteca Marciana, the Humanities Room, Wilson Library, University of North Carolina, and Dr. Carlo Revelli of the Biblioteche Civiche di Torino.

[93]

no uncertainty, for had not his grandfather in a final letter before dying instructed Charles to conquer Islam and to evangelize the antipodes? To a Europe that had seen in the past two decades the materialization of a new world beyond the seas conjoined with the results of Habsburg nuptial diplomacy that piled crowns and soon hereafter the imperial title upon Charles of Burgundy in such a way as to stagger the contemporary imagination, the new ruler awakened grave anxieties as well as boundless hopes. But to the courtiers and humanists who pressed around Charles, the device of Marlianus betokened the drive to universal Christian empire. It was at once a pledge and an aspiration.[2]

To appreciate the excitement and the foreboding that the young Habsburg prince awakened, we need to remind ourselves of the current mental outlook that allowed men to experience themselves as participants in a prophetic scheme of history. It is well known that medieval religious and political prophecy had received its ulti- mate stamp under the influence imparted by the twelfth-century Calabrian abbot, Joachim of Flora. Here was to be found the idea of that progressive trinitarian elaboration of world history, culminat- ing in the Age of the Spirit with its profound sense of *renovatio*, renewal. The Joachimite pattern juxtaposed the greatest earthly beatitude and the greatest tribulation, and in its development looked to an outstanding ruler, a monarch of the whole world, a second Charlemagne, repeatedly identified either with a current French Rex Christianissimus or with a German Rex Romanorum who would renew the church, chastise its ministers, conquer the Turk, and—like David—gather all sheep into one fold. Some ex- positors of the Joachimite tradition believed that an angelic pope, a *pastor angelicus*, shunning temporal goods and collaborating with the Savior-Emperor, would rule the Holy See. The astrologer- prophet Johann Lichtenberger represented one of the most recent and well-known expressions of this cast of thinking. In his *Prog- nosticatio* of 1488 he awaited the appearance of a Burgundian world emperor who would arise as a Second Charlemagne, the prince and monarch of all Europe, in order to reform the churches and the clergy. Throughout this vast literature that captured the historical imagination of successive generations and that associated grave foreboding with great hope, there moved as a continual refrain a single text in which profound anxiety gave way to joyous release, the text of John 10:16: "et fiet unum ovile et unus pastor."[3]

On that September day in 1517, he who embodied Habsburg destiny and represented for many the Savior-Emperor, had left behind in the Charterhouse of Scheut outside Brussels, forgotten and apparently removed from further political assignments, the man who would soon orchestrate the various themes of imperial *renovatio*, reform, and world order adumbrated by poets and humanists into a vast scheme of Ghibelline realization. But the events of the autumn of 1517—whether the departure of Charles for Spain or the posting of theses by a Saxon monk—seem to have left Mercurino Arborio de Gattinara irrevocably behind on the sidelines of the developing imperial drama. Scion of local nobility in Piedmont, product of a stiff juristic training and of almost a decade as a successful, even renowned, lawyer in Turin, champion of a most exalted appreciation of the law, Gattinara had distinguished himself by his zeal in the service of the Habsburg dynasty[4]. As chief architect of the notorious League of Cambrai against Venice, as a negotiator for the Archduchess Margaret and the Emperor Maximilian in a number of capacities, and as president of Burgundy since 1508, Gattinara had sacrificed every waking moment to the advancement of the dynasty. His rigorous application of Roman law in the province of Franche-Comté against a fractious nobility and his inflexible manner had produced such turmoil there that the Habsburg praetorian prefect of Burgundy, as he was inclined to envisage himself, had witnessed in these past months the erosion of both his personal finances and his political support. His relentless and brilliant services to the Habsburgs had prevented his fulfilling a vow, taken in 1513 and commuted by the pope, which had now brought him to the Charterhouse of Scheut in August of 1517 where he was to remain for the next seven months.[5] To his enemies in Franche-Comté as well as to those in the archduchess's government at Malines—and probably to himself—Gattinara's career as diplomat, administrator, and principal magistrate for the Habsburgs was over.

In his autobiography Gattinara later mentions how in the first month of his withdrawal to the monastery of Scheut he composed a small book, dedicated to Charles and designed to be presented to him before his departure. In this treatise Gattinara hailed the future monarchy of the world and the triumph of the Christians in the person of Divus Carolus, and he predicated supreme monarchy for Charles. Of this treatise only a fragment, a highly apocalyptic fragment, has survived. We can only surmise its contents.[6] But there can be no doubt as to its spirit and intent. The fallen magistrate was swept up in the current mood of apocalyptic expectation and imperial aspiration. In the charged atmosphere of the moment his sources were ready at hand. Nevertheless, it may be noted that Gattinara was a friend and reader of Jean Lemaire de Belges, the former court chronicler of Margaret.[7] In his treatise on the schisms and councils of the church Lemaire had warned that in the twenty-fourth and last schism secular princes would be constrained to undertake the reform of the clergy as proved by several prophets, sibyls, astrologers, holy persons, and mathematicians. He proceeded to quote them and, while mentioning Abbott Joachim, he drew most heavily upon Johann Lichtenberger.[8]

Having already suffered deposition from office, Gattinara emerged from his meditation and penance at Scheut in May 1518.[9] On his way homeward he apparently entertained notions of entering the service of his original master, Duke Charles of Savoy. But he was never to reach his destination. For in Spain Charles's grand chancellor, Jean Le Sauvage, had died in June; this second most important office at court and the one that was at the bureaucratic center of government needed a skilled jurist and experienced administrator. The gravity of the problem did not end here. In Germany, the aging emperor and in the Netherlands his gifted daughter Margaret, who embodied the imperial aspirations of the dynasty, must both now attend to the future election of a Habsburg to the Holy Roman Empire.[10] The narrow Flemish nationalism of Chièvres, who as grand chamberlain was the most prominent person in the entourage of Charles, could not provide the necessary vision of and justification for a world empire.[11] The archduchess and the emperor knew their man. Despite his recent fall from office, the ex-president of Burgundy's preeminent legal knowledge, his awesome capacity for work, and his absolute devotion to the dynasty were never in doubt and made him the only logical candidate.[12] On 15 October 1518 Mercurino de Gattinara took the oath of office between the hands of Charles in Saragossa.

In the ensuing twelve years up to his death the new "Grand Chancellor of all the realms and Kingdoms of the King"[13] would count for more than any other single person in the entourage of Charles. The relationship between the aged, experienced dynastic servant and the young emperor, which needs to be defined and elaborated beyond the picture so splendidly drawn by Karl Brandi, cannot concern us here. Neither can the reorganization of the Spanish central administration, nor the immense diplomatic activity of these years deflect us from our course. We seek the possibly less ambitious and more ambiguous task of defining and assessing the contours of a mind and a policy that can best be referred to as Ghibellinism. In a splendid article on Charles V and the idea of empire Frances Yates has noted among a number of sixteenth-century litterateurs the main features of Ghibelline aspiration: namely, the renewal of the empire, the emergence of an ideal master of the world, and the reign of justice and peace in a new golden age.[14] But what proves fruitful in the case of poets and philosophers will not suffice in the case of a statesman whose advice and policies were to be of paramount significance for European politics in this period. Thus without forsaking entirely the categories of Dr. Yates, we propose to study Gattinara's Ghibellinism under three broad topics: the educing of the idealized emperor; the reduction of the pope to his properly pastoral office; and the place of Italy in the emerging world *monarchia*. None is exclusive and all are so interrelated as to make it difficult to consider one without the other two.

Among the innumerable tasks confronting Gattinara on his arrival in the Iberian peninsula, the most subtle and absorbing was the portrayal of an emperor who would draw not only the youthful Habsburg but also his Spanish subjects to the vocation of empire. The first formal opportunity occurred with the need to respond publicly to the ambassadors of the German electors who brought the news of Charles's election as Holy Roman Emperor. On 30 November 1519, St. Andrew's Day, the patron saint of Burgundy, the grand chancellor delivered the speech of acceptance at Molina del Rey. The divinely inspired election of Charles, we are told, signified the restoration and renewal of the empire hitherto diminished and almost effaced. With the renewal of *sacrum imperium* the

Christian Commonwealth may receive necessary care, the Christian religion be increased, the Apostolic See stabilized, and the enemies of Christians exterminated so that the promise of the Savior that there will be one sheepfold and one shepherd may be fulfilled. God has indeed shown his favor that the empire divided under Charles the Great to the extent that most of it was overrun by enemies of the Christian religion is now able to be reestablished under Charles the Greatest and be led back to the obedience of the true and living pastor himself. Justice and peace embrace.[15]

In the first of those many *consultas* or memoranda whereby Gattinara sought to educate his master for the great opportunity that spread out before him and to advise him on all political matters, the grand chancellor reacted to the news, hardly a week old, that Charles had been elected Holy Roman Emperor:

Sire: God the creator has given you this grace of raising you in dignity above all Christian kings and princes by constituting you the greatest emperor and king who has been since the division of the empire, which was realized in the person of Charlemagne your predecessor, and by drawing you to the right path of monarchy in order to lead back the entire world to a single shepherd. Thus it is very reasonable that your imperial and Caesaric Majesty, in order to avoid the vice of ingratitude, should recognize his Creator as true distributor of all goods rendering to him appropriate thanks and attributing to him due praise by eschewing all ambition and vainglory . . . as well as those temptations and vices which might distract and repel [your] exercise of virtues and good works.[16]

Gattinara evidently felt responsible for the moral upbringing of the prince, a presumption that would not make any easier his relationship to Charles, and although he never had the time nor probably the desire to compose a *Speculum principis*, the equivalent can be deduced from successive *consultas*.

In pursuing his task Gattinara warns Charles that the exalting of the Christian faith, the growth of the Christian Commonwealth and the preservation of the Holy See, all for the attainment of universal peace, will be impossible without monarchy.[17] After correlating peace and monarchy, he then raises the theme that would be the continuing preoccupation of a lifetime of dynastic service—justice.

For the administration of that justice which is the queen of all virtues by which emperors, kings and princes rule and dominate, as God has given you the title of emperor and legislator and as it belongs alone to you to declare, interpret, correct, emend, and renew the imperial laws by which to order the entire world, it is most reasonable that in following up the suggestions (*vestiges*) of the good emperor Justinian, your Caesaric Majesty should early select the most outstanding jurists that one may find to undertake the reformation of the imperial laws and to advise on all possible means for the abbreviation of trials and for presenting such clear laws that the entire world may be inclined to make use of them and that one may say in effect that there is but a single emperor and a single universal law.[18]

Placing Justinian as a model before the emperor, Gattinara cites the contemporary jurist Celsus to the effect that the emperor is the vicar of God in his empire in order to accomplish justice in the temporal sphere.[19] He is the prince of justice.[20] The Dantesque vision of a jurist-emperor, who is the guardian and expositor of Roman law and who as *dominus mundi* champions justice and the law by a sort of preeminent moral and juridical authority but does not impose them by force, had received further support during the fourteenth century in the teaching of Bartolus.[21] This vision is now resurrected. Together with peace, justice completes the two great correlates of Augustine—*justitia et pax*—vital to Gattinara's view of universal monarchy.[22]

The response of Castilians to Charles's acceptance of the imperial office was almost totally negative. Whatever exhilaration and pride some *letrados* and humanists might have felt at the awareness of their king's being emperor was inevitably stifled by the profound anxiety that it produced among Charles's new subjects. And although Gattinara could not have been alone in urging the acceptance,[23] even if the royal council as early as 5 September 1519 had moved to proclaim that the title and office of emperor would not be exercised to the prejudice of Charles's Spanish kingdoms,[24] the question of Castile's new role in a world empire coupled with the abrupt departure of their king for Germany led directly to the revolt of the *comunidades*. In the Crown of Aragon, however, matters were different. Indeed, the town counselors of Barcelona, on hearing the news of their king's coronation at Aachen in 1520, enthusiastically responded in a remarkable Catalan proclamation wherein they hailed Charles as another Charlemagne, who, in using their city as the staging base for those expeditions that would recover Jerusalem, would subjugate the Turk, unite the two empires, the eastern and western, achieve the unification of the churches, Catholic and Orthodox, and realize a golden age wherein the lion would lie down with the lamb—ideas long nursed by readers of Ramón Lull.[25]

National opinion in both Castile and Aragon would ultimately be able to tolerate Charles's addition of the imperial dignity to his many crowns and dominions by claiming the emperor to be richer in Spain than in Germany and by respecting the providential mission of Charles as protector of Christendom.[26] Although this careful cultivation of the feeling of the Hispanic peoples is most evident in the imperial addresses to successive *cortes* after Charles's return in 1522, his departure from Spain in 1520 required the attention of both royal council and chancellery.[27] Among the papers constituting part of the personal file of Gattinara at the Biblioteca Reale in Turin is one, written in a fine humanist hand, that shows signs of having been circulated within the chancellery or possibly the royal council for revisions and additions before it appeared in its published form under the title *The Address of Charles, King of the Romans, in the Spanish Cortes, immediately before his Departure*. The tract constitutes a Latin reworking of the heart of the famous speech by Pedro Ruiz de la Mota, bishop of Badajoz, to the *cortes* of Santiago de Compostela on the early afternoon of 31 March 1520. The Latin tract is more compressed than the Castilian speech; the address has been shifted from the third to the first person with the king directly speaking; and while the development of the argument in the tract generally follows that of Mota's speech, the classical examples and emphases are different. Apparently directed toward that literate Spain beyond the immediate *procuradores* gathered at Santiago and designed to mollify the rising passions of Charles's Castilian subjects, the work could hardly have appeared in print without Gattinara's approval and, indeed, his direct participation. The existence of the manuscript together with the final Latin printed version and even a later German version demands a reconsideration of Mota's famous speech as a collective enterprise on the part of the royal council.[28]

As for the content of the Turin manuscript, empire, we are told, is not attained by whim or ambition but is bestowed by God alone. Charles here claims that the empire of Spain with its far-flung European possessions and with another, a gold-bearing world attached, would have sufficed, but the pressure of the Turk and the needs of religion as well as the welfare and dignity of his Spanish realms demand that he add Spain to Germany, the name of Caesar to that of Spanish king. Rome would have never had her empire if she had not sent forth men equal to the task. He promises to return to Spain, the citadel, staging base, and support of his kingdoms. The manuscript ends on the heroic note that while other peoples serve pleasure and utility, Spain alone is born to honor—to live and die for honor.[29]

In Gattinara's representation of the emperor to that monarch himself and to his Spanish subjects the messianic note is tempered by a moral concern feeding on classical models and examples that show the influence of humanism. Just as Dante in those letters that hailed the advent of the Emperor Henry VII in Italy applied to the ostensible Savior Emperor scriptural texts properly pertaining to the Messiah, likewise Gattinara since his early years in Habsburg service had exercised the same practice. In 1514 he had identified the Emperor Maximilian and the protection he must afford his daughter and grandson with the eagle of Deuteronomy 32:11 tending her young and John 10:30: "I and the Father are one." Repeatedly in the autobiography he clothes the emperor and his providential mission in these hues.[30] In accordance with earlier Ghibelline practice reminiscent of the Hohenstaufen chancellery, the sacralization of the imperial office perilously approaches the blasphemous. Yet in the *consultas*, where he directly addresses the emperor, the moral strain is uppermost. Gattinara never tires of drilling into the still impressionable mind of Charles the importance of an emperor's exercising justice, clemency, magnanimity, fortitude, liberality, and temperance, or of presenting models of Greek and Roman emperors.[31] In a remarkable series of articles that Gattinara circulated among the members of the Council of State early in the winter of

1523–24 for their criticism and reactions, under the rubric *amour des subjects*, the grand chancellor set forth one of his most used and favorite texts drawn from Seneca's *De clementia*: that for a ruler his subjects' love constitutes an impregnable fortress. In enjoining his master how he must present himself, be seen and known by his subjects, Gattinara encourages Charles to go into the churches, pass through the towns, and even go into the fields, entering into honest conversation with his people.[32] Although the aged chancellor's moral instruction and exhortation would in the long run wear on Charles so that the monarch would always breathe more freely during Gattinara's absences, nevertheless they left their impress upon the victor of Pavia, the conqueror of Tunis, so that his modesty and *gravitas* raised Charles head and shoulders above the deportment of his royal contemporaries. For our purposes here it should be noted that Gattinara conceived the moral stature and *providentia*[33] of the emperor as vital to the pacification of Spain, following his return in 1522, and vital also to providing the links between the emperor and other lands within the far-flung *monarchia*. In his idealized understanding of the Holy Roman Empire and the presently envisaged monarchy of the world Gattinara conceives of it less as a legal and administrative construct and more as something depending upon moral stature.

> Sire, your grandeur and the security of your affairs do not consist in holding Milan nor other states which hereafter you would be able to conquer and master, but it consists in winning the hearts of men and causing through them that kings, dukes, princes and potentates come to your devotion and obedience and recognize you as overlord. This is the way by which the Romans and others had the monarchy of the world, the remnants of which you ought to follow in order to attain thereto.[34]

A second aspect of Gattinara's Ghibellinism is his attitude toward the pope. The pope is considered chiefly a political and administrative figure—the ruler of the Papal States, the grantor of *cruzadas* and taxes upon the clergy so valuable to late medieval secular authorities. As with many notables in pre-Tridentine Europe before Luther began to draw attention to the papacy, Gattinara participated in a broad current of belief that saw the pope preeminently in political terms and sought to reduce him to his originally pastoral office. Nevertheless it would be a major misconstruing of

Gattinara's personality and career as chancellor to view him as religiously indifferent or as making religious issues the mere instruments of political ends. He was the first of Charles's counselors to assert the need for a council. The papal nuncio at Worms, Aleander, himself the epitome of a politicised ecclesiastic, saw Gattinara and Chièvres as using the issue of Luther to gain political ends. Yet while Chièvres thought that the whole Luther disturbance could be handled, Gattinara was impressed by its popular dimensions and saw the necessity of a council.[35] His frequent recourse to monastic retreats, his enthusiastic support of Erasmus as the preeminent teacher of the orthodox faith and as a middle way, his continuing desire to see the life of the clergy reformed—all argue for a seriously experienced catholicism that was neither Roman nor papal.[36]

Gattinara was ready enough to withstand any effort on the part of the pope to intervene in secular matters while advancing the claims of his imperial master to intrude upon the realm of the spiritual. In 1522 he continued to support Juan Manuel, the imperial ambassador at Rome, despite the determined campaign of Pope Adrian to get rid of him. Reading over the diplomatic correspondence, Gattinara grumbles, "The pope will content himself with what is reasonable and leave it to us to ask advice of whom we like."[37] When he drew up the instructions for Miguel de Herrera as special envoy to Italy and to the pope in November 1525 his tone becomes more menacing: "[Tell] His Holiness that if he does not want to use his office of common pastor for the tranquility of Italy and of Christendom, then we will be forced to use our office as emperor, and His Holiness ought to take note that we still have in our hands the King of France and that he is in our power to leave when we wish it."[38]

The imperial victory at Pavia in February 1525 encouraged Gattinara to urge the emperor, shortly after the receipt of the news, to make the pope call a council to extirpate the errors of the Lutheran sect, reform the affairs of Christendom, and mobilize effective action against the Turk. If the pope should excuse himself, then the emperor as *advocat et protecteur* of the church should undertake the convoking of a council.[39] As the diplomatic situation darkened and the conniving of Pope Clement with France and sundry Italian states threatened to remove the imperial grip upon the peninsula, Gattinara's insistence that Charles seize the initiative became more strident. In July 1526 he composed one of his longest *consultas*. Therein he urged the emperor to realize the goal of one sheepfold and one shepherd by going to Italy and by convoking a council for the reform of the church and the extirpation of heresies. He would subject the Lutherans to the truth of evangelical doctrine in which he believed, the sect to be for the most part grounded, win them over as much as possible by amnesty, clemency, and pardons, and thus turn with renewed strength against the Turk.[40]

Amidst the deepening diplomatic crisis the grand chancellor found an outstanding spokesman for his ideas in the person of Alfonso de Valdés, who had been a permanent scribe in the imperial chancellery since 1521 and became one of its Latin secretaries in 1526.[41] Under the direction and guidance of the Council of State and the grand chancellor, Valdés had been entrusted with the task of composing the official government report on Pavia. Therein Valdés identified the Spaniards as the elect people of God and presented the imperial victory as releasing Charles to attack the Turks and the Moors, recover the empire of Constantinople, and retake the Holy Sepulchre in Jerusalem, thus fulfilling the words of the Redeemer, "Fiet unum ovile et unus pastor."[42] Now with the slipping of Pope Clement VII back into the French orbit and the materialization of the League of Cognac, Gattinara was able to look to Valdés's stalwart assistance in leading the diplomatic offensive against Pope Clement during the summer and fall of 1526.

In the remarkable replies that were delivered over to the papal nuncio Baldassare Castiglione at Granada, 17 and 18 September 1526, if the hand proclaimed the work of Valdés, the voice was clearly that of Gattinara.[43] In a conscious effort to obtain the understanding and approval of secular and ecclesiastical princes, magistrates and citizens throughout the Habsburg empire, the grand chancellor arranged to have the correspondence between pope and emperor together with related materials published at Alcalá, Antwerp, Cologne, and Mainz.[44] The first imperial reply to Clement and the letter to the Sacred College of Cardinals interest us here. The former letter, while raking up all past wrongs inflicted by Rome upon Charles, repeatedly finds the pope neglectful of his pastoral duties, which is another way of saying that he is deeply involved in preparations for war directed against the very one who is the most obedient prince in all Europe and seeks only the good of Italy.[45] Rather than a shepherd and a mediator, the pope has become a wolf, a partisan, a begetter of war. The letter reaffirms those *duo luminaria* both instituted by God that should rule cooperatively, bring peace to Christendom and war against the Turk. It concludes on the menacing note that if the pope refuses to exercise his responsibilities as a father and pastor, the emperor must have recourse to a general council, which he now begs the pope to convoke for healing the wounds of Christendom.[46] Pressing the point still further, the imperial chancellery on 6 October dispatched a letter to the College of Cardinals, asking it to call a council if the pope demurred.[47] The consternation that these letters created in Rome was dulled only by the sack of the city itself.[48] And as the imperial propaganda campaign reached its crescendo, Gattinara for good measure tried to enlist the efforts of the prince of humanists to publish a definitive edition of Dante's *De monarchia*.[49] But Erasmus's view of Christian polity was not that of Gattinara, and the *editio princeps* of Dante's work would have to wait three more decades before another spectacular clash between emperor and pope promoted its publication.[50]

More important than the refusal of Erasmus was the caution and reluctance of the emperor concerning the conciliar policy of his minister. Although a council for Gattinara was an obvious means of realizing necessary ecclesiastical reform, as well as a political lever to embarrass a vacillating pope, Charles was probably more realistic in recognizing the highly sensitive nature of the conciliar issue; either wisely or out of native Habsburg dilatoriness he refused to be rushed along. In actual fact, his own interest in a council did not permit resort to such extremes, and it is quite possible that the conciliar issue contributed to the rupture between the emperor and his chancellor that occurred in March 1527.[51]

The reasons for Gattinara's withdrawal from government and trip to Italy were complex and a long time in maturing. Although these reasons cannot concern us here, one is relevant to the present issue. There is some evidence that his belief in the imminence of the *pastor angelicus* drew him to Italy at this time.[52] When he arrived in Monaco, the chancellor was greeted with the news of Rome's sack by the imperial army. Unable to refrain from his customary task, so recently relinquished, of counseling the emperor, Gattinara promptly sat down to communicate his advice in this instance. In his autobiography he tells us that he presented the emperor with two alternatives: either Charles could approve the deed, the pope being not the pastor but the robber, disturber, and waster of Christendom, having assumed arms for himself and turned a deaf ear to the imploring requests for a council; or, if he could not accept the rigor of this advice nor condone the actions of his soldiers, Charles could proclaim his horror of the event and manifest his desire for a peace and the submission of his case to a general council. In actual fact, what Gattinara wrote to the emperor on this occasion, included amidst a series of recommendations and directions, was that His Majesty must purge himself of blame before all Christian princes; that Valdés must write good Latin letters and in them ask for the convocation of a council to heal divisions and extirpate heresies. While awaiting a response, the emperor should make his own preparations for a council. Gattinara concluded that with a victorious army in Italy the emperor would be on *le droit chemin de la monarchie*.[53]

Gattinara's suggestion to the emperor may have served as the initial impetus that led to Valdés's composition of his notorious dialogue on the sack of Rome. With his customary enthusiasm the chancellery's Latin secretary, entering into the spirit of things, asserted at the end of the *Lactancio* dialogue that Christ founded the church and the emperor restored it.[54] If the passionate Valdés proved to be more Erasmian than Erasmus, it could also be said that his Ghibelline zeal sometimes exceeded that of his master, Gattinara.[55] Although it is doubtful that the chancellor himself would have gone so far as to equate the emperor with Christ regarding their services to the church, he was ultimately responsible for the entertainment of such an idea within the imperial chancellery. Likewise, it is also doubtful that he would have gone so far as his cousin, Giovanni Bartolomeo di Gattinara, the emperor's leading negotiator at Rome, who in writing back to Charles casually inquired what sort of Apostolic See, if any, ought to remain in Rome and how it ought to be maintained other than entirely under the control of the prince.[56] Gattinara participated in that world of thought and policy that had not yet experienced the impact of Luther's reformation upon the papacy.[57] At the same time he belonged to more than a century of political experience that recognized that ultimately more could be gained in cooperation with the pope than in opposition and more specifically that pope and emperor, papacy and empire, needed each other. Thus it is not surprising that Gattinara should write during this same period that if the pope should come to Spain to negotiate, he, Gattinara, would eagerly return to do business.[58] Although the pope himself did not go to Barcelona in 1529 to negotiate, his legate did, and the resulting treaty of Barcelona brought to an end Gattinara's express anti-Romanism and conciliarism and, in effect, thereby undercut his own Ghibellinism.

Italy and its role within the *monarchia* constitute the final aspect of our inquiry into Gattinara's Ghibellinism. To Dante Italy was the garden of the empire, to Petrarch a land most holy destined to be the mistress of all the world, and to Paolo Giovio, the contemporary historian of Charles V's reign, she was that infallible ladder of true monarchy. Nor did one have to be a Ghibelline to admire Italy's centrality within Christendom. A century after Giovio, Richelieu would allow in his *Political Testament* that Italy was deemed the heart of the world and the preeminent part of the Spanish empire.[59] By the beginning of the sixteenth century Italy had become the decisive arena for the clashing ambitions and rival claims of Valois and Habsburg. On first coming to the office of chancellor and continuing throughout the succeeding decade Gattinara in all his *consultas* drummed into his master's ear that Italy was the principal foundation of his empire, and lacking it, his honor was void and the growth of his empire jeopardized. He who would counsel ignoring Italy, counseled the emperor's shame and ruin.[60] Repeatedly over the years Gattinara urged Charles V to come to Italy, secure his justice and order there, and complete the pacification of the land. When Gattinara speaks of Italy, he can mean the entire peninsula well known to the Roman jurist that he was, but he can also suggest the traditional notion of the *regnum Italicum*, which included only the north and central portions of the peninsula. For he frequently distinguishes Italy from Naples and Sicily and continually reverts to the problems of the comity of independent states north of the Neapolitan kingdom.[61]

Another distinctive feature of his attitude toward Italy is that this Burgundo-Piedmontese statesman has no feeling for Rome and its *Mystik*, which he seems to transfer to Italy as a whole. Rather than Rome, the cities of Milan and Genoa occupy his constant attention, and he never tires of insisting that they are together the gateway to Italy: the two duchies are the keys and bastions for keeping and dominating all Italy reduced to the emperor's subjection and as the seat and scepter for dominating the world.[62] Here he defined a strategic truth that made the Genoa-Milan axis the veritable hinge of the entire Habsburg position in Europe, an axiom that would be affirmed long after the chancellor had passed from the scene.[63]

How did Gattinara approach the problem of Italy's liberty, namely the independence of her city-states, which for his contemporary, Francesco Guicciardini, provided the social and political bases for Renaissance culture? The solution to the Italian riddle lay through Milan. He who controlled that city would be master of Italy. Gattinara steadfastly opposed the generals—Lannoy, De Leyva, Moncada, Pescara—who would seize Milan outright, impose a military solution upon the Italian problem, and reach an accord with France at the expense of Italy.[64] For this reason he brooked the emperor's wrath and refused to apply the seals of office to the treaty of Madrid on 14 January 1526. Instead he urged that the present duke, Francesco Sforza, be invested with the imperial fief of Milan and that the imperial army be reduced to a small effective force whose maintenance would not ruin the Milanese. By preserving this state in his devotion the emperor would accomplish more than by having a lieutenant hold it outright, for according to the chancellor, subjects are more inclined to employ their lives and property for the defense of their estate and their immediate lord when they know him to be on good relations with the emperor. Gattinara's reasons for propping up the existing regime in Milan stemmed from a more precise appreciation of the emperor's position with respect to the pope and Venice. To seize Milan would transgress treaties and understandings with both.[65] Gattinara's reliance upon a league and upon awakening native elements within Italy points to a looser and more general imperial hegemony.

Since the end of 1523 and with increasing urgency during and after the negotiations for the treaty of Madrid Gattinara advocated a union with the Italian states. Italy was in his mind always the center and basis of the Habsburg empire. "Italy is to be preserved for him more by love than by force and with their love he will be able to dominate all the world and without it His Majesty will thrust his kingdoms and affairs into peril and never will he be able to recover himself without necessity and work."[66] Once the emperor united with Italy, the pacification of his land might be extended to a general pacification within Christendom, which would bring the kings of England and France into an alliance against Turk and heretic.[67] In adjusting these two essentially opposing conditions—the independence of the Italian states and Italy's imperial role—Gattinara invoked the relationship between ancient Rome and her client states within the Holy Roman Empire.[68] He could warn that by using force rather than love and humanity, Rome had taken longer to master the rest of Italy than to conquer the world.[69]

Gattinara's appeal to the Roman Empire seems to have been fundamental to his solution to the Italian problem. Gasparo Contarini, after five years as Venetian ambassador to the imperial court, emphasized this feature in his *relazione* to the Senate. He distinguished the two rival parties within the imperial council, one led by Gattinara, the other by the Viceroy Lannoy. In characterizing the former, he says that the Romans, Cyrus, and others who have produced something like universal monarchies have nevertheless not ruled all directly but have had other kings and other friendly republics that have favored them, enjoying their fraternity. This was the way that the chancellor guided His Imperial Majesty.[70] The contemporary sources for the basis of his appeal to the Roman Empire lie beyond the scope of our present inquiry, but it can be observed that as a jurist trained in the Roman law Gattinara was doubtlessly aware of the *jus Italicum* that, developing out of the Republic and constituting a basic feature of the pre-Diocletian empire, extended the legal status of Italian cities to non-Italian provincial cities and communities; it comprised various rights of a public and private character such as self-government and exemption from supervision by the governor of the province.[71] Thus particularly for Italy and to some extent elsewhere *monarchia* connoted ideally not a uniformly organized empire but a looser Habsburg hegemony that would give room to local privileges, provincial customs, native institutions.[72]

It would be a mistake, however, to believe that Gattinara intended to apply in equal measure to all other lands and kingdoms in the *monarchia* the policy of clemency and relaxed guidance that distinguished his treatment of Italy. Although love, clemency, justice are the preeminent characteristics in the chancellor's conception of a world order, when dealing with a pronounced enemy and any allies of that enemy Gattinara reveals a more aggressive and oppressive drive in his thinking.

France represented the one discordant note in the existing political scene that prevented the rapid realization of Gattinara's Ghibelline dream. France blocked any mobilization of the Christian world on the part of the emperor for war against the Turk. More immediately, she had her own claims to Naples and to Milan. Gattinara nursed an invincible distrust of France, and the first step in his contribution to the emperor's diplomacy was to bring the papacy and England into the lists against France. By the treaty of Windsor, immediately preceding the court's departure for Spain in 1522, the allies agreed on a dismemberment of France. The idea of a virtual *Vernichtungskrieg* in the early sixteenth century may seem to cast a curious light on chivalric-dynastic politics.[73] Nevertheless, since the prevailing image of European polity at this time still was supremacy and empire rather than competitive balance, our shock is diminished and the high stakes for which Valois and Habsburg struggled become evident.[74] After the imperial victory at Pavia, Gattinara sought to realize that reduction of France whereby the emperor might regain his rightful possession of Burgundy, obtain a corridor through southern France, and remove forever the French grip from northern Italy. The chancellor recommended the Habsburg possession of Languedoc and Provence—an idea that was receiving some ventilation in the chambers of imperial government at the time. To obtain the legal arguments for affording the emperor this ready access to Italy, Gattinara undertook the ransacking of the archives at Barcelona.[75] Three years later, after his return to court and power, Gattinara in the midst of a bitter struggle with France and England composed a *consulta* predicated on a false report concerning the death of the king of France. Gattinara called for the restoration of the empire to its original vigor with the reacquisition of Dauphiné, the Arelate kingdom, "y otras tales." Through the Dauphin, at the time his prisoner, the emperor would establish a sort of protectorate over France without destroying the kingdom. And under the guise of avenging Queen Catherine of England and her daughter, the emperor could take the island realm. In the midst of considering a Scottish alliance in order to implement such a design, Gattinara breaks off, interrupted by other work,—or by the truth that his great enemy still lived.[76] Despite its interest and its value for defining the aggressive element, at its most inflated, in Gattinara's conception of the *monarchia*, not much weight should be given the document. Probably written early in the winter of 1527–28, it belongs to what Fernand Braudel calls the time of bulging files, the winter plans, when the servants of government could concoct the most grandiose schemes, when, before the blazing hearth in the cozy chamber, no plan seemed too difficult, no policy too bizarre—all only to disintegrate before the harsh realities of the spring.[77]

In the construction of Charles's monarchy the special care that Gattinara directed toward Italy and her imperial role supports his claim that he was an Italian, seeking the liberty of Italy.[78] *Libertà d' Italia*—the words appear repeatedly on the lips and quills of the leading Italian political thinkers and actors during those very years that saw the death agony of that independence usually signified by the phrase and that had made the Italian Renaissance possible. Both Gattinara's Florentine contemporaries Machiavelli and Guicciardini could agree with him in perceiving a vital connection between the destiny of Milan and the liberty of Italy. Yet both could now strenuously oppose the Habsburg *monarchia d' Italia* as they had earlier opposed French domination.[79] However marginal an Italian Gattinara might be and whatever his tangled motives, he appeared to some Italians as one trying to moderate the impact of foreign domination upon the peninsula. The papal nuncio to Castile, Baldassare Castiglione, writing to the archbishop of Capua, could observe that no one in Spain had such a good mind for Italian affairs as Gattinara.[80] Contarini, who often had some caustic comments to make about Gattinara, could remark that he was a second Joseph in that both had the opportunity to benefit their people—Joseph, the Hebrews and Gattinara, the Italians.[81] He did not disguise his relief when in July 1525 Gattinara's resignation was refused, and he considered the chancellor's return to the Council of State a reason for all Italians to rejoice.[82] For his own part Gattinara could afford to represent himself to Contarini as ready to dare all for the liberty and welfare of Italy.[83] Prematurely in 1522 he could claim the merit of having freed his country from the barbarians.[84] And ever on the prowl for funds to support the insatiable war machine, reducing its numbers and its pillaging to effective control, Gattinara could approach Contarini as a fellow Italian and in his efforts to obtain a contribution from Venice, express his deep desire to remove the ruinous Spanish soldiery from the country.[85]

In the supreme crisis of the Italian Renaissance that culminated in the sack of Rome *libertà d' Italia* had a variety of meanings according to the minds of the leading protagonists. Insofar as he could realize and maintain it during the few years remaining to him, Gattinara's accommodation was certainly the most realistic, the most practical; apart from Italy's role in his Dantesque theory of empire, Gattinara squarely confronted the problem of adjusting his land to the facts of Spanish might and the French menace. In this respect Castiglione was more perceptive of current political realities than were his two Florentine contemporaries.[86] The solutions of Machiavelli and Guicciardini either failed to materialize or were shattered by events. Gattinara, the child of both Dante and Bartolus, strove to construct a broad enough conception of monarchy to allow for those two poles around which Italy's life continued to move—universalism and particularism.[87] By the treaty of Barcelona, 29 January 1529, the emperor capitalized on the recent destruction of the French army before Naples and his alliance with Genoa and the fleet of Andrea Doria—an alliance for which Gattinara had provided the groundwork and impetus.[88] The treaty, described by contemporaries as Gattinara's masterpiece, provided for the decisive accommodation between emperor and pope. And while it sounded the death knell of the Florentine republic, it led to

the General League of Italian States realized at Bologna at the end
of the year. Gattinara, by then a dying man, accompanied his
master to Italy, received his long-desired cardinal's hat; months
later Charles received the imperial crown from Pope Clement at
Bologna. As the emperor and his suite moved northward toward
Germany, the mood that settled upon Italy, according to Benedetto
Varchi, eyewitness and historian of these events, was one of in-
credulous relief:

> For [the emperor] had succeeded not as barbarously as people had
> imagined, [judging from] the cruelty done by his ministers and soldiers,
> but most consummately and very benignly and even beyond the believing
> of many had returned the State of Milan to the duke. It was thought by
> some . . . who had observed his manners and actions that it had not been
> by chance and without art that he had so pleasingly caressed all and had
> sought with such industry and benevolence to oblige all who were able to
> aid or impede his enterprises.[89]

The pacification of Italy was the last and greatest service that Gattinara rendered his master. Not without its uncertainties and ambi-
guities, this Spanish domination of the peninsula would be secured
by the treaty of Cateau-Cambrésis thirty years later and would
endure for a century and a half.

The treaty of Barcelona destroyed the recrudescence of Ghibellinism that we have tried to define here. But Gattinara's Ghibellinism, which attempted to integrate notions of the ideal emperor,
antipapalism, and the central role of Italy into an overall conception
of world empire, evaporated not because it was unrealistic or ir-
relevant or even successfully contested but because much of it
could be attained through other means—by cooperation with the
pope. To our own age the illusion of empire seems the grandest of
all at the beginning of what is traditionally considered the modern
period. In his pursuit of explaining the present out of the past, the
historian of this period all too often becomes mesmerized by the
apparently triumphant march of the "national state" to the neglect
of those other polities, the city-state and the conception of empire
as a broad hegemony, both of which are treated as so much political debris. And yet in their time it was this that Valois and Habsburg
struggled to obtain, the supreme magistracy of Europe—this the
reality, this the goal. Neither a phantom nor a mirage, empire

conceived as a leadership of Europe, a broad hegemony steadied by the presence of the Ottoman threat, was later to receive sufficient realization in Spanish diplomacy, bureaucracy, and armed might to hypnotize a century of French statesmen.

In conclusion, any assessment of Gattinara's conception of empire would need to note that it was not so doctrinaire as to be incapable of change during the twelve years of his chancellorship. In this respect the revolt of the *comunidades* seems to have had a salutary effect not only upon Gattinara but also upon other members of the imperial government in making them realize the limits of the possible in the politics of their age. Gattinara's early vision of a uniform law and uniform justice came to be tempered by an enforced respect for native institutions and customs and the value of the *cortes*.[90] On the other hand, the orientation of his view of empire remains firmly focused on Europe and appears quite unaffected by the American experience and Castile's presence in the New World. That the chancellor shared this basic blindness with his contemporaries becomes astonishing only when we reflect that here was a man who knew and had dealt directly with Hernán Cortes; who was a friend and correspondent of Peter Martyr of Anghiera, the first historian of America; and finally who had worked intimately with and given decisive support to Las Casas in his efforts to reform the government of the Indies.[91] Third, Gattinara's idea of empire is essentially moral, legal, and fully capable of admitting national differences; there is no distinction between the concept of universal monarchy and Christian empire.[92] Finally, in his preoccupation with empire, as it applied to an essentially Romanic world, the juristic elements, composing his view of universal monarchy, seem to recede behind eschatological and prophetic ones. In the last months of effective work, Gattinara's mind strained beyond the immediate negotiations with the pope to that final mobilization of Christendom under the emperor's leadership in a crusade against the Turk.[93]

The contemporary prophetic-eschatological understanding of history caused Europeans to experience themselves as participants in a cosmic drama, not as observers in an impersonal process. And 1529–30 can be designated the most apocalyptic year of the sixteenth century. During the autumn of 1529 Suleiman's hordes advanced upon and besieged Vienna. The Ottoman cataclysm, which could be understood only in universalist terms, sent tremors throughout Europe and convulsed the humanist community. Erasmus, quite expectably, composed the least apocalyptic and the most reluctantly bellicose tract among those that flooded from the press. His *Consolation concerning the Turkish War together with an Exposition of Psalm 28* was the last work ever to be read by Gattinara.[94] More vehement and disturbed was Juan Luis Vives, outstanding proponent of peace and concord among Christian princes, who now rejected any accommodation and urged common action against the Turk.[95] From a cardinal of the church came a remarkably Ghibelline response to the mounting crisis of the age. In his vast historical enterprise, the *Scechina*, completed in 1530 and addressed to the emperor, Giles of Viterbo saw Charles V as the new Cyrus who would cleanse the church; the true king of Jerusalem, who would shepherd the flock into one fold; the church's advocate and even messiah in the struggle against Islam.[96] In a similar vein, the Spanish humanist and Aristotelian, Juan Gines Sepúlveda, product of Bologna and resident at Rome, had greeted Charles's appearance in Italy with an *Exhortation—to War against the Turks* in which he summoned the emperor to that most holy and sacred war, to that task most befitting the office of *imperator*, whereby Jerusalem and "all the remaining lands of the earth might be added to the power and most holy religion of Christians."[97]

During these same months came from the presses of Wittenberg in Saxony a number of tracts bearing upon war and the Turk, culminating in a *Military Sermon* of a very different nature indeed from that of Sepúlveda's *Exhortation*. Martin Luther fully experienced the apocalyptic nature of the moment; at no time in his life was he so certain of the imminence of the world's end as in late 1529 and early 1530.[98] Nevertheless, in calling upon Germans and Europeans to accept the leadership of the emperor in war against the Turk, Luther drove home a distinction that would prove a fatal blow to empire itself. In accordance with his profound belief that Christians were not so many that they could get together in mobs (say nothing of armies), Luther insisted that the subject obey his ruler in war against the Turk but that this duty was not to be understood as part of a crusade, not a holy enterprise, and the emperor should undertake its leadership simply as a secular ruler and not as some sort of universal head or vicar of Christendom.[99] Implicit here is that unraveling of the essential bonds of empire, similar to that already occurring in the ecclesiastical sphere. For despite the trivial witticism of Voltaire, the traditional empire was holy—its sacral character evident in Roman law, in an anointed ruler, and in that ruler's special role as champion of the church. To deny this role, to reject holy war and make crusade into just another secular struggle, had the effect of decisively advancing the disintegration of the Holy Roman Empire. Luther and Sepúlveda—two worlds in irreconcilable conflict!

But when the two Habsburg brothers, Charles and Ferdinand, met in the Tyrol and conferred at length far into the spring, while the diet summoned to Augsburg anxiously awaited their attendance, none could have surmised that process of disintegration soon to be released within the *Reich*: the formation of an independent political league, the consolidation of the territorial church, confessional strife, foreign intervention, and at the end that bitter moment before Metz where the imperial motto *Plus Oultre* had to withdraw before the besieged, who flaunted in conscious defiance the counterdevice of an imperial eagle chained to the Herculean columns with the inscription *Non Ultra Metas*—"not beyond these limits," not beyond Metz.[100] It was May 1530, the high noon of the Habsburg empire in Europe. As the cardinal lay dying at Innsbruck, the true dimensions of the crisis of empire lurked obscurely in the immediate future. When on 5 June Charles's great minister closed his eyes upon the world, who could have said with certainty that an accommodation might not yet be made with the Lutheran specter and that Europe might not be drawn closer to the realization of one sheepfold, one shepherd?

NOTES

1. The following abbreviations are used throughout the notes to this paper: Bibl. Marc.—Biblioteca Marciana; BMB—Bibliothèque municipale de Besançon; BR—Biblioteca Reale di Torino; BRA—Bibliothèque Royale Albert Ier; HHSA—Haus-, Hof- und Staatsarchiv.

2. On Marlianus and the columnar device of Charles V see the excellent article of Earl E. Rosenthal, "The Invention of the Columnar Device of Emperor Charles V at the Court of Burgundy in Flanders in 1516," *Journal of the Warburg and Courtauld Institutes* 36 (1973): 198–230.

3. What follows in this paragraph is indebted to the magisterial study of Marjorie Reeves, *The Influence of Prophecy in the Later Middle Ages: A Study in Joachimism* (Oxford, 1969), esp. pp. 350, 365, 386–87, 431, 447, 507, and passim.

4. The first study of Gattinara appears to have been a Kiel University dissertation of the eighteenth century, written by Philip Frederick Hane, which constitutes a part of his *Historia sacrorum* (Kiel, 1728) that was intended to serve as a highly schematized *Handbuch* for the systematic representation and study of Protestant church history. In accordance with the Melanchthonian tradition Gattinara was here presented as a would-be Protestant. I am indebted to Dr. Birgitte Hvidt of Det Kgl. Bibliotek, Copenhagen, for a reproduction of its copy, that of Kiel University Library having been destroyed in the last war. The Munich University Library has a Leipzig, 1729 copy, 4⁰ H. eccl. 1969 (2). In March and May 1753, M. de Courbezon read two papers to the Academy of Besançon on Gattinara (BMB, MS 1102, vol. 2, fols. 402–31; and Fonds de l'Academie, MS 5, fols. 131v–42). There followed Carlo Tenivelli's "Vita di Mercurino da Gattinara," an unpublished manuscript composed in 1781 and read in the Accademia di Torino on 12 December 1782 (BR, Misc. 114.6). The first real biography of Gattinara was that of Carlo Denina, *Elogio storico di Mercurino di Gattinara Gran Cancelliere dell' imperadore Carlo V e cardinale di S. Chiesa*, Piemontesi Illustri, Vol. 3 (Torino, 1783), which still has merit. Only in the nineteenth century did a number of limited studies of Gattinara begin to appear: M. Huart, *Le Cardinal Arborio de Gattinara Président du Parlement de Dole et chancellier de Charles-Quint* (Besançon, 1876); M. Le Glay, "Études biographiques sur Mercurino Arborio di Gattinara," *Société royale des sciences . . . de Lille. Memoires* 31 (1847): 183–260; Gaudenzio Claretta, "Notizie per servire alla vita del Gran Cancelliere di Carlo V., Mercurino di Gattinara," *Memorie della reale accademia della scienze di Torino* 47 (1897): 67–147 and Gaudenzio Claretta, "Notice pour servir à la vie de Mercurin de Gattinara, Grand Chancelier de Charles-Quint d'àpres des documents originaux," *Société savoisienne d'histoire et d'archéologie* 37 (1898): 245–344. Both Le Glay and Claretta are important for the documents published therein. The event that raised the history of Gattinara's career above the local and obscure and placed it in the main current of historical scholarship was the publication of his autobiography and related documents at the beginning of the twentieth century by Carlo Bornate. See Carlo Bornate, ed., "Historia vite et gestorum per dominum magnum cancellarium . . . con note, aggiunte e documenti," *Miscellanea di storia Italiana* 48 (1915): 233–568. (Hereafter this work will be cited in the following fashion: the autobiography itself, Bornate, "Vita;" the annotations, Bornate, "Noti;" the completion of the autobiography which itself extends only until August 1529, Bornate, "Aggiunte;" several important memoranda and some correspondence, Bornate, "Documenti.") Since Bornate's publication a number of outstanding historical works have given a significant, even crucial role, to Gattinara: Karl Brandi, *The Emperor Charles V*, trans. C. V. Wedgwood (London, 1954); Marcel Bataillon, *Érasme et l'Espagne* (Paris, 1937); Manuel Giménez Fernandez, *Bartolomé de Las Casas*, 2 (Seville, 1960); and Fritz Walser, *Die spanischen Zentralbehörden und der Staatsrat Karls V* (Göttingen, 1959). Although quite incom-

plete, the best bibliography for Gattinara can be found in Karl Brandi, *Kaiser Karl V.* 2 vols. Vol. 2, *Quellen und Erörterungen* (Darmstadt, 1967), p. 43.

5. P. De Wael, "Collectanea rerum gestorum et eventuum Cartusiae Bruxellensis," 1625, (BRA call number 7043), vol. 1, fol. 157v; Joan. Bapt. de Vaddere, "Historia monasterii nostrae dominae de gratia," Anderlac 1691, (BRA call number 11616), fols. 145–49. Concerning the pressure applied on Margaret to dismiss Gattinara from his office as president of Burgundy, see her letter of May 1518 to the Duke of Savoy, published in Max Bruchet, *Marguerite d'Autriche, Duchesse de Savoie* (Lille, 1927), pp. 407–8. Gattinara's presidency was made further untenable by a complicated lawsuit in which he was himself the defendant. The case provides a splendid example of the operations of justice in the early sixteenth century and has been recognized as such and examined with care only by Andreas Walther, *Die burgundischen Zentralbehörden unter Maximilian I und Karl V* (Leipzig, 1909), pp. 30–38. Walther's assessment, however, relied upon the archives of the Grand Council at Malines without reference to or knowledge of Gattinara's own account in the autobiography and papers in the Gattinara family archives at Vercelli. Cf. Bornate, "Vita" and Bornate, "Noti," pp. 256–66. Although the case very much involved the purchase and forced resale of the Chevigny estate by Gattinara, there is ample evidence that the trial had its political reverberations in Franche-Comté and in the Netherlands government at Malines.

6. Bornate, "Vita" and Bornate, "Noti," pp. 266–67.

7. The correspondence between Gattinara and Margaret of Austria published in L. M. G. Kooperberg, *Margaretha van Oosterrijk, Landvoogdes der Nederlanden, tot den vrede van Kamerijk* (Amsterdam, 1908), pp. 357–58, cf. p. 343, reveals Gattinara's interest in the reception of one of Lemaire's latest works. In the prologue to his *La concorde du gendre humain* (Brussels, 1508), written to honor the conclusion of the peace of Cambrai by Margaret, Jean Lemaire writes: "A noble et magnifique personne Messire Mercurin des seigneurs de Gattinaire docteur en tous droitz. Conseillier de Lempereur, de Larchiduc et de madame leur fille et tante. Et leur president de la conte de Bourgoigne et du pays de Bresse Jehan Lemaire." M. E. Kronenberg, *Nederlandsche Bibliographie van 1500 tot 1540*, 2 ('S-Gravenhage, 1940), no. 3375.

8. Jean Lemaire de Belges, *Oeuvres*, edited by J. Stecher (Geneva, 1969), 3:351–55.

9. On the dating of Gattinara's stay at Scheut I am here following De Wael and HHSA (Belgien), PC 72, fols. 9–10, which is a copy of the act of destitution dated 22 February 1517 (1518). Margaret's letter to the duke of Savoy, May 1518 (see n. 5 above), speaks of the event as having occurred in the recent past. But cf. Le Glay, "Études," pp. 208–10, which dates Gattinara's leaving Scheut as May 1517. At Malines and Dole the new year began at Easter.

10. On the leading role played by Margaret in the imperial election and the background to Gattinara's appointment as grand chancellor see the important work of Walser, *Die spanischen Zentralbehörden*, pp. 141–42. Published posthumously, this work has been reorganized, supplemented, and completed by Rainer Wohlfeil, who in places is as much the author as Walser.

11. On this point see Andreas Walther, *Die Anfänge Karls V* (Leipzig, 1911), pp. 186–87 and the chapter on Chièvres.

12. Walser, *Die spanischen Zentralbehörden*, pp. 161–63; see also the letter of Margaret to Maximilian of 1513 in M. Le Glay, ed., *Correspondance de l'empereur Maximilian Ier et de Marguerite d'Autriche . . . 1507–1519*, 2 vols. (Paris, 1839), 2:243–44.

13. Brandi, *Emperor Charles V*, p. 90.

14. Frances A. Yates, "Charles Quint et l'idee d'empire," *Fêtes et Cérémonies au temps de Charles Quint*, IIe Congrès de l'Association internationale des Historiens de la Renaissance (Paris, 1960), p. 64.

15. Both the copy of the *Responsiva oratio* in the Bibliothèque Nationale and that

in Luxembourg Bibliothèque Nationale being unavailable, that printed in Hane, *Historia sacrorum*, pp. 58–60 was used here:

ut divino satisfiat obsequio, Reipublicae consulatur, sacrum Imperium restauretur, Christianae religioni incrementum accedat, Apostolica sedes stabiliatur, ipsa Petri navicula diu fluctuans, in salutis portum de[d]ucatur: perfidorum quoque Christiani nominis hostium exterminatio sequatur, hincque Salvatoris sententia impleatur, ut fiat unum ovile, & unus pastor . . . Quid praeterea laudabilius iis adscribi posset, quam quod ex ipsa praeteritarum, praesentium & futurarum rerum animadversione eum Imperatorem futurum decernerent, qui diminutum ac fere exhaustum Imperium restaurare posset, qui implumem Aquilam refoveret, renovaret, ac ad propriam naturam deduceret . . . Faxit itaque Deus optimus maximus, ut hujusmodi Imperium sub Carolo magno divisum, & ut plurimum a Christianae religionis hostibus occupatum, sub Carolo Maximo valeat instaurari, ad ipsiusque vivi & veri pastoris obedientiam reduci.

Cf. Kronenberg, *Nederlandsche Bibliographie*, 2, no. 3369.

16. Bornate, "Documenti," pp. 405–6. On the date upon which Charles received the news of his election see his letter to the viceroy of Cerdeña in Manuel Fernandez Alvarez, ed., *Corpus Documental de Carlos V.* (Salamanca, 1973), 1:81.

17. Bornate, "Documenti," p. 406.

18. Ibid., p. 408.

19. Walser, *Die spanischen Zentralbehörden*, p. 174.

20. Bornate, "Documenti," p. 507.

21. Cf. Dante *De mon.* 1.11–14. Except for one parallel not treated by Brandi, the present author has intentionally avoided considering specific influences of Dante on Gattinara, which can be found in the excellent article by Karl Brandi, "Dantes Monarchia und die Italienpolitik Mercurino Gattinaras," *Deutsches Dante-Jahrbuch* 24 (1942): 1–19. On Bartolus's appreciation of the emperor's power rather than as expositor of particularistic sovereignty see Jan Baszkiewicz, "Quelques remarques sur la conception de Dominum mundi dans l'oeuvre de Bartolus," (Bartolo da Sassoferrato. II Studi e documenti per il VI Centenario) *Convegno commemorativo del VI centenario di Bartolo* (Perugia, 1959), pp. 9–25.

22. Cf. Aug. *De civ. dei* 19. 12–28. In his remonstrance to the Emperor Maximilian of September 1514, entitled "Remonstrances de Messire Mercurin de Gatinare [*sic*], President de Bourgongne faictes à Maximilian I Empereur sur les traverses causées à sa personne et au Parlement par le Marschal de Bourgongne" (BMB, Collection Chifflet, t. 187, fols. 116–34). Gattinara twice quotes the famous *Remota iustitia* . . . (*De civ. dei* 4. 4) and draws a fairly extensive passage from Augustine's treatment of Psalm 84(85): 11, cf. Aug. *Enarr. in Ps.* 84, Corpus Christianorum 39. 1172. ll. 14–20. I am here dependent upon a late sixteenth- or early seventeenth-century copy of the "Remonstrance," fols. 127v, 133, and 120. I wish also to take the opportunity to thank Mme. O. Paris and the staff of the Bibliothèque municipale de Besançon for making this material available to me; the manuscript is important with respect to Roman law and humanism and is being prepared for publication.

23. According to Mota's speech (see below) the election was accepted, "mas con el parescer de todos los grandes y perlados, caballeros y personas del su Consejo que en su corte se hallaron, que no solo lo aconsejaron pero firmaronlo de sus nonbres." *Cortes de los antiguos reinos de León y de Castilla*, La Real Academia de la Historia, 5 vols. (Madrid, 1882), 4:294. Walser, *Die spanischen Zentralbehörden*, p. 142, would support the belief that behind the hard-won unanimity, ultimately presented by the royal council, was more than just the sole initial vote of Gattinara for the acceptance, as the chancellor would have us believe from his autobiography. Cf. Bornate, "Vita," pp. 272–73.

24. Alonso de Santa Cruz, *Crónica del emperador Carlos V*, edited by Ricardo Beltrán y Rózpide and Antonio Blázquez y Delgado-Aguilera, 5 vols. (Madrid,

John M. Headley

1920–25), 1:204; Juan Beneyto Perez, *España y el problema de Europa: Contribución a la historia de la idea de imperio* (Madrid, 1942), pp. 253–54.
    25. Quoted in Joan Reglà Campistol, *Introduccio a la Historia de la Corona d'Aragó. Dels origens a la Nova Planta* (Palma de Mallorca, 1969), pp. 102–4.
    26. Ricardo del Arco y Garay, *La idea de imperio en la politica y la literatura españolas* (Madrid, 1944), pp. 135–36. Cf. Beneyto Perez, *España*, pp. 216, 231.
    27. Brandi, *Quellen*, pp. 153–54; Walser, *Die spanischen Zentralbehörden*, p. 178; and the important collective *consulta* composed by Gattinara to the emperor at the end of 1523 printed in the appendix, Ernest Gossart, *Espagnols et Flamands au XVIe siècle: Charles Quint roi d'Espagne*, (Brussels, 1910), pp. 245–46.
    28. Here is not the place for an exhaustive analysis and conclusive identification of BR, St. d'Ital. 75 (Miscellanea politica del secolo XVI), but the following general points may be made to suggest that it preeminently constitutes a fragment of Gattinara's chancellery files: forty-three separate items (39.9 percent of the total material) can be immediately identified as by, to, or read by Gattinara, according to the address, marginal comments, or endorsement; forty-eight separate items (32.1 percent) can be associated with him as ambassadorial instructions, relevant political affairs, communications of his cousin Giovanni Bartolomeo Gattinara to the emperor, copies of treaties that would be likely for reference, along with the splendid exposition of the office of grand chancellor composed apparently at Gattinara's request and for his benefit by the Audiencier Philippe Hanneton (fols. 683–86v; cf. Claretta, *Notice*, p. 312); twenty-seven separate items (25.5 percent) appear more removed but still belong to the period and might well have constituted part of Gattinara's system of reference; nine separate items (2.5 percent) derive from the decades immediately after Gattinara's death and must have been bound into the *mazzo* at a later date, perhaps in the nineteenth century. (Cf. also below, nn. 38 and 75). BR, St. d'Ital. 75, fols. 569–70 is written in a fine humanist, roman hand that would suggest the work of the Latin secretaries, Gaspar Argillense or Sanchez de Orihuela. (Cf. Luis Nuñez Contreras, *Un registro de cancellería de Carlos V. El MS 917 de la biblioteca nacional de Madrid* [Madrid, 1965], p. xxix). The changes in the draft appear to be stylistic; what seems to be another hand has written "pene alio orbe," then crossed out "orbe" and completed the rendering of "con otro nuevo mundo de oro fecho para él" (*Cortes*, 4:294–95) from the original with "aurifero orbe," (fol. 569v). The published Latin version reveals a considerable number of stylistic changes beyond the draft, and although it includes those changes and additions made in the draft it has a concluding section the manuscript for which is lacking. This manuscript may well have become separated and lost from the present *mazzo*, BR, St. d'Ital. 75. I have used here the Münchner Universitäts bibliothek copy, 4 Hist. 2580, entitled *Caroli Ro [manorum] Regis Recessuri adlocutio in conventu Hispaniarum*. Only two known copies exist in the United States: one at Harvard designated as "Rome, J. Mazochius, 1519" and the second at the New York Public Library designated as "Augsburg? 1520?" I have not yet been able to consult the New York copy, but the Munich version constitutes a separate edition quite distinct from that identified by Harvard as Mazochius's. The catalog of the Bibliothèque nationale (26:1049) not only indicates the presence of a copy of the Latin publication but also a German one (cat. no. Mp. 1570). Upon inspection the latter would appear to derive from the press of Michael Hillen in Antwerp if the banderole on the title page bearing the letters MHAV can be so credited. The "aurifero orbe" passage is here rendered "unnd eyner andern/also tzu reden guldene welt" sig. [Av]. Antonio Palau y Dulcet, *Manual de librero hispanoamericano* (Oxford-Madrid-Barcelona, 1950), 3:172, tentatively suggests Augsburg as the place of publication for the Latin version but gives the impossible date 1518. Late 1520 or early 1521 would be more likely. But more important to know is the place of publication of the Munich copy, which must wait upon an analysis of watermarks and other bibliographical evidence. Another level

of analysis that needs to be pursued before we can gain greater insight into the authorship of the speech attributed to Mota and into the public image that the royal-imperial council sought to project is a close examination of the literary sources and overall content of the speech. Menéndez Pidal has pointed out the use of Claudian (XXX [XXIX] *Laus Serenae*, ll. 64, 66) *[Hispania] contulit Augustos. . . . haec generat qui cuncta regant* for the idea that while other lands may be rich in material resources, Spain produces world rulers. Ramon Menéndez Pidal, ed., *Historia de España* (Madrid, 1966), 18:xxviii. With the recrudescence of the imperial theme during these years the late Roman imperial poet enjoyed renewed attention. Although it cannot be argued that any one person exercises a monopoly over the citing of an earlier author, particularly at a time of revived interest in that author, it is worth noting that in his Remonstrance of 1514 (see above, n. 22) Gattinara had drawn two passages from Claudian's *Panegyricus de quarto consulatu Honorii Augusti* (ll. 276–77, 267–68; cf. BMB (Coll. Chif.), t. 187, fol. 131v) for quotation. Of Mota's classical interests, on the other hand, we know nothing except that he was adept at several languages. But to keep this largely circumstantial evidence in proper perspective, Peter Giles in his panegyric celebrating the entry of Charles into Antwerp in 1520 will quote the same passages from Claudian in the same reverse order (*Hypotheses sive argumenta spectaculorum*; [Antwerp, 1520], sig. [bii]; cf. sig. ci). As it is most improbable that Giles had ever seen Gattinara's manuscript, it would seem that both secretary and chancellor drew from a common secondary source. In the same line of argument, one may note in the ostensible speech of Mota the following statement: "ya sabeis que asy como no es menos virtud conservar lo ganado que adquerirlo de nuevo, asi no es menor vituperio no seguir la victoria, que ser vencido" (*Cortes*, 4:295), which seems to have its root in the very common Latin proverb *Non minor est virtus quam querere, parta tueri* (Hans Walther, ed., *Lateinische Sprichwörter und Sentenzen des Mittelalters* [Göttingen, 1963–67], no. 18042; cf. no. 5200) that Gattinara develops at some length again in his "Remonstrance" (fol. 125v). Furthermore, it may be observed that the particular designation of America as a "new gold-bearing world" seems to have had some currency in the circles of the imperial chancellery, for in August 1521 as leading member of Charles V's delegation to the Calais conference, Gattinara composed a public denunciation of Francis I's politics, wherein he stated that by equipping his fleets, the emperor propagated the dominion of Christ *in novo aurifero orbe*. Pierre de Vaissiere, ed., *Journal de Jean Barrillon*, 2 vols. (Paris, 1899), 2:227. Finally, to sum up, we are merely arguing here that the authorship of the speech attributed to Mota may be collective and in its several redactions a product of the royal council. At least the question needs to be considered in the light of this possibility. For even the best Spanish historians Mota's speech has tended to become one of the great vested interests of Spanish historiography: Jose Antonio Maravall, *Carlos V y el pensamiento politico del renacimiento* (Madrid, 1960), p. 112, while accepting Mota's speech at face value, can argue without any apparent reason that Gattinara's speech to the cortes of Valladolid in 1523 represents a collective enterprise. We merely suggest here that on better grounds the reverse may be argued.

29. BR, St. d'Ital. 75, fol. 570: "meminerit caeteras gentes voluptati et utilitati servire solam hispaniam ad honorem natam pro honore et vivere posse et mori." In the Latin printed edition this passage appears at sig. Aiiv. Here as in all other cases throughout this article the manuscript and typographical abbreviations will be silently expanded.

30. See the remarks of A. P. d'Entrèves, *Dante as a Political Thinker* (Oxford, 1952), pp. 37 and 51, on Dante *Ep.* 5 and *Ep.* 7. 2 (Toynbee ed.) On Gattinara, BMB, (Coll. Chif.) 186, fol. 128v and Bornate, "Vita," pp. 323, 325, 356, 363.

31. Bornate, "Documenti," pp. 408–9.

32. Gossart, *Espagnols et Flamands*, pp. 245–46. Cf. Seneca *De clem.* 1. 19. 6: "Unum est inexpugnabile munimentum amor civium."

33. On *providentia* as exercised by Roman emperors see M. P. Charlesworth, "The Virtues of a Roman Emperor," *Proceedings of the British Academy* 23 (1973): 105–33, esp. 118 ff. Gattinara does not use the term itself, but the notion is present. On the religious and particularly chivalric background to the formation of Charles V's moral character and the previous influence of such persons as Chièvres, Margaret, Glapion, Adrian of Utrecht, see the suggestive remarks by Carlos Clavería, *Le Chevalier Délibéré de Oliver de la Marche y sus versiones españolas del siglo XVI* (Zaragoza, n.d.), pp. 48–50, 68–69.

34. Gossart, *Espagnols et Flamands*, pp. 250–57.

35. Paul Kalkoff, *Die Depeschen des Nuntius Aleander vom Wormser Reichstage 1521* (Halle a. S., 1897), pp. 102, 112; A. Wrede, ed., *Deutsche Reichstagsakten unter Kaiser Karl V*, Jüngere Reihe (Gotha, 1896), 2:521, 827.

36. Bornate, "Vita," pp. 263–66, 343, 354. Cf. P. S. Allen et al., eds., *Opus epistolarum Des. Erasmi Roterodami*, 12 vols. (Oxford, 1906–58), 4:479. Cf. also Vaddere, "Historia Monasterii," on his exemplary conduct at Scheut.

37. See G. A. Bergenroth, ed., *Calendar of Letters, Despatches and State Papers relating to the Negotiations between England and Spain* (London, 1866), 2:375 (hereafter cited as *SP Span.*).

38. BR, St. d'Ital. 75, fol. 39v: "el dicho duque [Sessa] y vos como devos mismos sin mostrar de tener comission de nos sobrello, de dezir a su santidad que no queriendo su santidad de usar de officio de comun pastor por la quietud de ytalia y de la cristiandad que ental caso seriamos forcado usar de nuestro officio como emperador y que su santidad debria pensar que tenemos ahun en nuestras manos el Rey de francia y que es en nuestro poder de saltar lo quando querremos y usando con el de liberidad y dexando nos delo que le havemos pedido fazer lo nuestro amigo." The editors of *SP Span.* apparently ignored Herrera's Instructions (fols. 37–40v), together with other relevant materials to be found in this *mazzo*.

39. Karl Brandi, "Nach Pavia: Pescara und die italienischen Staaten, Sommer und Herbst 1525," Berichte und Studien zur Geschichte Karls V., 17, *Nachrichten von der Gesellschaft der Wissenschaften zu Göttingen*, Philologisch-Historische Klasse (1939), pp. 202–3; cf. Bornate, "Vita," p. 348. See also Hubert Jedin, *A History of the Council of Trent* (London, 1957), 1:227–28, 240–41 for Gattinara's use of a council.

40. Bornate, "Documenti," 502–3: "se assossegaran en alguna forma los dichos tumultos de allemagna: y los culpados de haver sostenido y favorecido los dichos errores de luthero . . . se podran assegurar y mas facilmente retirarse de los dichos errores; especialmente dandoles camino con que rectamente se pueda determinar la verdad de la doctrina evangelica en la qual principalmente se funda la dicha secta."

41. Andreas Walther, "Kanzleiordnungen Maximilians I, Karls V, und Ferdinands I," *Archiv für Urkundenforschung* 2 (1909): 388; Marcel Bataillon, *Erasmo y España* (Mexico, 1966), p. 231.

42. Sigs. Aviiv–Aviiiv. The collective authorship of the report on the battle of Pavia and of similar public statements of the imperial government stemming from the chancellery is evident from the title of the Pavia tract: *Relacion delas nuevas de Italia sacadas delas cartas que los capitanes y comisario del Emperador y Rey nuestro señor han escripto a su magestad: assi dela victoria contra el rey de Francia come de otras cosas alla acaecidas: vista y corregida por el señor gran Chanciller y consejo de su magestad.*

43. Ibid., pp. 335–37. But cf. Bornate, "Vita," pp. 332–33. The detailed legal and diplomatic knowledge evident particularly in the first reply to Clement VII points to Gattinara as both presiding over and participating in the production of that double compilation entitled *Pro Divo Carolo eius nominis quinto Romanorum Imperatore Invictissimo, pio, felice, semper Augusto, Patrepatriae, in satisfactionem quidem sine talione eorum quae in illum scripta, ac pleraque etiam in vulgum aedita fuere, Apologetici libri duo*

nuper ex Hispanis allati cum alijs nonnullis, quorum catalogos ante cuiusque exordium reperies (Mainz: Joannis Schoeffer, 1527). (This is the definitive edition.)

44. *Pro Divo*, p. 1. The imperial propaganda campaign of 1526–27 deserves separate, extensive treatment. The main features can only be mentioned here. According to the colophon the first to appear was the Cologne edition (March 1527) *Epistolae duae altera Clementis VII . . . altera Karoli*, which included only the first of Clement's two letters and Charles's reply (Bibl. Marc. Miscell. 2451.5). The Miguel de Eguía edition (Alcalá, April 1527) included all materials bearing on the controversy between emperor and pope except the very brief second letter from Clement. I have consulted copies both in BMB (Coll. Granvelle) and HHSA (Belgien), PA 94, fols. 1–40v. The Antwerp editions are numerous: a Latin edition by Joannes Graphaeus including both the French and the papal controversies (19 August); the same in Dutch (12 September); a Latin edition of the French controversy by Michael Hiller (August); a Latin edition of the French controversy by Marten de Keyser (1527); a French edition of the same by Willem Vorstermann; then two Latin editions of 1527 that include both controversies: *Pro Carolo V apologetici II* jointly by Gottfried Dumaeus and Marten de Keyser and another by Joannes Graphaeus identical with his first. See Kronenberg, *Nederlandsche Bibliographie*, 1–3, nos. 1263, 1266, 1264, 1265, 1269, 3297, and 0721, respectively. As privileged printer to the chancellery of the empire at Mainz, Joannes Schoeffer was the obvious agent for the purveying of these materials within the *Reich*. Cf. F. W. E. Roth, "Die Mainzer Buchdruckerfamilie Schoeffer," *Beihefte zum Centralblatt für Bibliothekswesen 9* (Leipzig, 1892): 3–11. Parts of the two controversies would enjoy reprintings in the course of the century and the several parts constituting the Mainz edition can be found distributed through Melchior Goldast's *Politica imperialia* and *Collectio constitutionum imperialium*. On the financing of the Eguía edition see Bataillon, *Erasmo y España*, p. 230.

45. *Pro Divo*, pp. 32, 76.

46. Ibid., pp. 77–80, 84.

47. Ibid., pp. 98–99.

48. The papal reaction to the materials in *Pro Divo* can be followed in Bergenroth, *SP Span.*, 3/1:1039, 1045–47, 1056–58, 3/2:8–9, 37–42, 76–77.

49. Allen et al., *Opus epistolarum*, 6:470–71.

50. For the political and literary background to the publication of the *De monarchia* and its German translation, see the valuable study of Andreas Burckhardt, *Johannes Basilius Herold. Kaiser und Reich im protestantischen Schrifttum des Basler Buchdrucks um die Mitte des 16. Jahrhunderts* (Basel and Stuttgart, 1967), pp. 194–212. Burckhardt disputes the suggestion made by Peter Bietenholz that the manuscript of the *De monarchia*, presumably sent by Gattinara to Erasmus, served as the basis for printer's copy.

51. On the different positions taken by Gattinara and the emperor concerning a council see Gerhard Müller, "Zur Vorgeschichte des Tridentinums: Karl V und das Konzil aährend des Pontifikates Clemens' VII," *Zeitschrift für Kirchengeschichte 74* (1963): 87, 91–94. Although in the opinion of the present writer Müller is correct in distinguishing between the two developing positions, he errs in attributing to Gattinara purely political motives.

52. J. S. Brewer, James Gairdner, and R. H. Brodie, eds., *Letters and Papers, Foreign and Domestic, on the Reign of Henry VIII* (London, 1862–1932), 4/2, no. 4977.

53. Bornate, "Vita," p. 348; HHSA (Belgien), PA 94, fols. 451–52v; cf. Brandi, *Quellen*, p. 185.

54. Alfonso de Valdés, *Diálogo de las cosas ocurridas en Roma*, ed. José F. Montesinos (Madrid, 1969), p. 155.

55. For a presentation of Valdés that emphasizes the influence of Gattinara rather than of Erasmus, cf. Sosio Pezzella, "Alfonso de Valdés e la politica religiosa di Carlo V," *Studi e Materiali di storia della religioni 36* (1965): 211–68, esp. pp. 223, 265–68.

56. Brandi, *Quellen*, p. 182.

57. Cf. Bergenroth, *SP Span.*, 4:195–201, 209–10, 235–38.

58. HHSA (Belgien), PA 94, fol. 446: "Et qui si avant mon embarquement survenoit nouvelle certaine de la venue du pape en barcelonne je me detiendroye illeques pour non faillir au service de votre maieste en telle coniuncture."

59. *Par.* 6. 105; T. Neri, G. Martellotti, E. Bianche, N. Sapegno, eds., *Francesco Petrarca. Rime, Trionfi e Poesie Latine* (Milan/Naples, [1951]), p. 804, "Ad Italiam"; Paolo Giovio, *Epistolae*, ed. Giuseppe Guido Ferrero (Rome, 1956), 2:10; on Richelieu see Hermann Weber, "Richelieu und das Reich," in *Frankreich und das Reich im 16. und 17. Jahrhundert* (Göttingen, n.d.), p. 39.

60. Bornate, "Documenti," p. 429.

61. Cf. Claretta, *Notice*, p. 323: Remonstrance of 1523 to Charles; Gossart, *Espagnols et Flamands*, p. 250; *Cortes*, 4:348: to the *cortes* of 1523 Gattinara says that the fall of Rhodes allows the Turk to threaten "sobre Napoles e Italia." Cf. also F. de Laiglesia, *Estudios históricos 1515–1555*, 3 vols. (Madrid, 1918), 1:367 for the continuation of this cortes in 1524: where Gattinara speaks of the kingdoms of Naples and Sicily and "todos los potentados de Italia." On the medieval understanding of Italy in connection with the notion of the *regnum Italicum* see B. H. Sumner, "Dante and the *Regnum Italicum*," *Medium Aevum* 1 (1932): 22–23.

62. Gossart, *Espagnols et Flamands*, pp. 250 ff.; cf. the original HHSA (Belgien), PC 68, fol. 22–22v, which indicates general agreement within the royal council.

63. See Alva's advice in Federico Chabod, "¿ Milan o los Países Bajos? Las discussiones en España sobre la 'alternitiva' de 1544," *Carlos V (1500–1558). Homenaje de la Universidad de Granada* (Granada, 1958), pp. 345–64, 369–70; also idem, *Storia di Milano nell' epoca di Carlo V*, Fondazione Trecanni degli Alfieri ([Torino, 1971]), pp. 55–56, 101–7 and passim where the emphasis falls upon the centrality of Milan.

64. Federico Chabod, *Lo stato di Milano nella prima metà del secolo XVI* (Roma, 1955), p. 26; Eugenio Albèri, ed., *Relazioni degli ambasciatore venete al senato*, 2 vols. (Firenze, 1840), 2:57; Brandi, "Nach Pavia," p. 219.

65. Gossart, *Espagnols et Flamands*, pp. 250–57.

66. Bornate, "Documenti," pp. 463–69: *consulta* Sept. 1525.

67. Ibid., p. 462: *consulta* Sept. 1525.

68. Gossart, *Espagnols et Flamands*, p. 257.

69. Bornate, "Vita," p. 307.

70. Albèri, *Relazioni*, p. 59.

71. Adolf Berger, "Encyclopedic Dictionary of Roman Law," *Transactions of the American Philosophical Society*, n.s. 43/2 (1953): 530.

72. Brandi, "Nach Pavia," p. 151. Cf. also Bergenroth, *SP Span.*, 2:517, for Gattinara's favorable reaction to the pope's support of Siena's independence, while urging it in December 1522 to pay annually a certain sum to the emperor in recognition of his suzerainty.

73. Cf. John Lynch, *Spain and the Habsburgs: Empire and Absolutism*, 2 vols. (New York, 1964), 1:80.

74. Cf. Michel François, "L'idée d'empire en France sous Charles-Quint," *Charles-Quint et son temps*, Colloques internationaux du Centre National de la Recherche Scientifique 30 September–3 October 1958 (Paris, 1958), p. 30, who quotes the Venetian ambassador Marion Cavelli in his *relazione* of 1546, concerning the differences that oppose France to Charles, that the bone of contention was not some particular state "ma ad un certo modo della superiorità ed arbitrio della Christianità." See also Giovio, *Epistolae*, 1:282 and Maravall, *Carlos V*, pp. 98–99.

75. Brandi, "Nach Pavia," p. 206. On the ransacking of the archives at Barcelona to equip Gattinara with legal arguments for the occupation of Languedoc and Provence there are scattered among the papers in BR, St. d'Ital. 75, which has been identified here as preeminently being part of Gattinara's personal working file, fols.

28–30v, 190–221v, materials under the title *Acta & documenta in authentica forma extracta ex regis archivis Barchinonae Comitatuum Civitatum, Terrarum, Castellorum, ac Jurium in Gallia per comites Barchinonae & deinde per Reges Aragoniae acquisitorum & post per plures annos possessorum ac consequentes ad Caesarem nunc gloriose Imperantem & Regna[n]tem spetantium [sic] et pertinentium.* Gattinara will draw upon these materials for his memorandum, written during the negotiations leading up to the treaty of Madrid, the French version of which appears in BR, St. d'Ital. 75, fols. 642–74v under the title *Informacion des droicts et querrelles de la maison de Bourgoinge [sic] contre France Sur les demandes faictes depuis La prinse du Roy de France pour parvenir a bonne paix.* The Latin version of this memorandum was published by Bornate, *Memoire de Chancelier de Gattinara sur les droits de Charles-Quint au duché de Bourgogne* (Brussels, 1907), which finds among its biblical citations John 10:16 and Psalm 84(85):11. Cf. Bergenroth, *SP Span.*, 3/1:93–94. See also HHSA (Belgien), PA 92, fol. 11 on the search through the Barcelona archives for legal claims to Languedoc.

76. HHSA (Belgien), PA 95, fols. 324–27, esp. 326v–27: "Si a este effecto queriendo su magestad apoderarse y assegurar del dicho reyno de Ingleterra: se hauria de hazer con color del desaffyo y por el drecho que su magestad puede iustamente pretender al dicho reyno: mejor que el rey que agora lo possee: por muchos cabos: o si sera mejor mostrar de hazerlo: por vengar la injuria de la reyna y para que la princessa su hija no quede bastarda: ny privada de la succession paterna: sin mostrar que su magestad quiera occupar el dicho reyno por si."

77. Fernand Braudel, *The Mediterranean and the Mediterranean World in the Age of Philip II*, 2 vols. (New York, 1973), 1:254. But cf. Bergenroth, *SP Span.*, 3/2:577–79, 878, 887 for the reality of this issue and the diplomatic mission of Cornelius Scepperus, Gattinara's subordinate and humanist friend, to Scotland.

78. Rawdon Brown, ed., *Calendar of State Papers and Manuscripts existing in the Archives and Collections of Venice 1520–1526* (London, 1869), 3, no. 401 (hereafter cited as *SP Venice*).

79. Chabod, *Lo stato*, pp. 8–16.

80. Carlo Bornate, "L'apogeo della casa di Absburgo e l'opera politica di un Gran Cancelliere di Carlo V," *Nuova Rivista Storica*, 3 (1919): 417.

81. Brown, *SP Venice*, 3, no. 956.

82. Ibid., no. 1064.

83. Ibid., nos. 401, 438; Ernest Gossart, "L'apprentissage politique de l'empereur," in *Espagnols et Flamands*, p. 196.

84. Brown, *SP Venice*, 3, no. 461.

85. Ibid., no. 1069.

86. Vittorio Cian, *Un illustre nunzio pontificio del Rinascimento Baldassar Castiglione*, Studi e testi, 156 (Città del Vaticano, 1951), pp. 126–28.

87. See the well-balanced and insightful article of Giovanni Barbero, "Idealismo e realismo nella politica del Gattinara, Gran Cancelliere di Carlo V," *Bollettino storico per la Provincia di Novara* 58 (1967): 3–18.

88. On Gattinara's continuing concern for Genoa and her role in the *monarchia* see Brown, *SP Venice*, 3, no. 746; Brandi, "Nach Pavia," p. 208; HHSA (Belgien), PA 91/3, fols. 258, 333v; PA 92, fol. 13; PA 94, fol. 470v; PA 95, fol. 326.

89. Benedetto Varchi, *Storia fiorentina* (Cologne, 1721), p. 355. "Lasciò l'Imperadore tutta l'Italia piena di grandissimo sospetto, perciocchè, sebbene egli era riuscito non mica barbaro, ed efferato, come se l'erano immaginato le genti, per le crudeltà fatte da Ministri, e soldati suoi, ma costumatissimo, e benigno molto, e sebbene aveva, oltre il credere di molti, renduto lo Stato di Milano al Duca, si conosceva però da chi vi badava che . . . i quali avevano osservato i modi, e l'azioni sue, che non fosse stato fatto a caso, e senz'arte l'aver elgi così piacevolmente accarezzato ognuno, e cercato con ogni industria, e amorevolezza di farsi benevoli, e obbiligati tutti coloro, i quali potevano, o aiutare l'imprese sue, o impedirle." On the appar-

ently conscious effort made by Spaniards at this time to ingratiate themselves with Italians and reduce the shock of Spain's dominance in the peninsula cf. Bergenroth, *SP Span.*, 4/1: 484–85, 568–69, 585.

90. See, for example, Gattinara's mid-October 1521 letter to the emperor, HHSA (Belgien), PC 4, fols. 181–181v, on Diego de Mendoza's coming as viceroy to Catalonia from Valencia, where he had gained a bad reputation. Gattinara manifests alarm that Mendoza, who needs to be bridled, is against the form of the constitution of the country and the privileges of the city of Barcelona, which he scandalizes. Published in Karl Lanz, ed., *Aktenstücke und Briefe zur Geschichte Kaiser Karls V* (Wien, 1853), Monumenta Habsburgica, Zweite Abteilung, 1:386–87. Cf. also Walser, *Die spanischen Zentralbehörden*, pp. 178–83.

91. On Europe's "mental shutters" coming down before the immense novelty of America see J. H. Elliott, *The Old World and the New 1492–1650* (Cambridge, 1970), chap. 1; on Cortes's relation to Gattinara see Antonio de Solis, *Istoria della conquista del Messico* (Venice, 1715), pp. 490–505; on Pietro Martyro Anghiera see his *Opus epistolarum Petri Martyris Mediolanensis* (Alcala, 1530), passim; on Las Casas see his *Historia de las Indias*, ed. Agustin Millares Carlo and Lewis Hanke (Mexico-Buenos Aires, 1951), 3:278–363 and Manuel Giménez Fernández, *Bartolome de las Casas* (Seville, 1960), 2: passim.

92. But cf. the well-known article by Ramon Menéndez Pidal, "La idea imperial de Carlos V," which first appeared in the *Revista Cubana* 10 (1937) and attained its definitive form as the preface to volume 18 of *Historia de España*, edited by the same author. For a good criticism, other than those of Brandi and Rassow, of Menéndez Pidal's distinction between *monarquía universal* and *universitas christiana* see Chabod, *Storia*, p. 132. See also the articles by Menéndez Pidal and J. Vicens Vives in *Charles-Quint et son temps*, Colloques internationaux du Centre National de la Recherche Scientifique 30 September–3 October 1958 (Paris, 1958), pp. 1–21 and the discussion therein. On Gattinara's recognition of national differences, see Walser, *Die spanischen Zentralbehörden*, pp. 171–74.

93. Bergenroth, *SP Span.*, 4/1:620. By *cruzada* Gattinara intends here the special indulgence tax authorized by the papacy, not "crusade" itself; but the diplomatic activity of these months with respect to obtaining support from England and France can be traced in Bergenroth, *SP Span.*, 4/1:279–80, 297–98, 307, 338–45, 397–98, 411–14.

94. J. Clericus, ed., *Desiderii Erasmi Roterodami opera omnia* (Leiden, 1704), 5:345–68, esp. pp. 367–68; see Allen et al., *Opus epistolarum*, 8:463, the important letter of Scepperus to Erasmus, 28 June 1530.

95. Carlos B. Noreña, *Juan Luis Vives* (The Hague, 1970), p. 225.

96. John W. O'Malley, *Giles of Viterbo on Church and Reform* (Leiden, 1968), pp. 116, 130, 176–77.

97. J. G. Sepulveda, "Ad Carolum V. Imperatorem invictissimum ut facta cum omnibus Christianis pace bellum suscipiat in Turcas, Cohortatio," *Opera, cum edita, tum inedita* (Madrid, 1780), 4:373–74: "Age igitur, Imperator felicissime, et omnes cunctandi moras abrumpe, omissisque his bellis, quae, si verum quaerimus, parum habent et emolumenti et dignitatis, optatissimaque pace Christianis reddita, ad haec propera, in haec toto animo et cunctis opibus incumbe, ad quae officium te Imperatoris vocat, pietas hortatur tum in patriam, tum in Deum et religionem, quae cum libertate et salute reipublicae Christianae . . . in summum discrimen adducitur . . . ut miseram Graeciam et finitimas Christianorum regiones cum Byzantio regia jam pridem Romanorum Imperatorum in libertatem asseras, et minoris Asiae opulentissimae regionis, et finitimarum gentium usque Mesopotamiam et Aegyptum imperio potitus, in sancta urbe Hierusalem teste nostrae redemtionis oculata . . . ut te Imperatore et bellum administrante, reliquus terrarum orbis ditioni Christianorum et sanctissimae religioni adjiciatur."

98. John M. Headley, *Luther's View of Church History* (New Haven and London, 1967), pp. 245–46.

99. *D. Martin Luthers Werke* (Weimar, 1909), 30/2:173–74, 189; cf. also 114, 130–31, esp. 130, ll. 27–28, which clash with Gattinara's statement to the cortes of Valladolid of 1523—"de que Dios nuestro Sennor merritisimamente le hizo Rey e sennor, e sobre los quales le elegió e constituyó su bicario y generalmente de toda la cristiandad, cuya universal cabeça es su Alteza," *Cortes*, 4:335.

100. On this point see Earl Rosenthal, "Plus Ultra, Non Plus Ultra, and the Columnar Device of Emperor Charles V," *Journal of the Warburg and Courtauld Institutes* 34 (1971): 216.

Appendix

Seminars of the Seventh Session of the Southeastern Institute
of Medieval and Renaissance Studies
30 June–8 August 1975

I. TRANSMISSION OF CLASSICAL AND LITURGICAL TEXTS IN THE MIDDLE AGES

Senior Fellow: Dr. Francis L. Newton, Professor of Latin, Duke University. Professor, Vanderbilt University (1953–67). President, Classical Association of the Middle West and South (1966–67). ACLS Fellow (1971–72). Editor, *Laurenti Monachi Casinensis, Archiepiscopi Amalfitani, Opera*, Monumenta Germaniae historica, Quellen zur Geistesgeschichte des Mittelalters, 6 (1973). Author, "Laurence of Amalfi's Mathematical Teaching," *Traditio* 21 (1965): 445–49; "Reconstructing the Monte Cassino Library of the Early Eleventh Century," *Yearbook of the American Philosophical Society* 1967, pp. 602–4; "Beneventan Scribes and Subscriptions. With a List of Those Known at the Present Time," *The Bookmark* 43 (1973): 1–35; "The Rediscovery of a Lost Monte Cassino Manuscript," *Quellen und Forschungen aus italienischen Archiven und Bibliotheken* 53 (1973): 457–58; etc.

Description: Studies in the paleography and textual history of classical and liturgical manuscripts. The seminar paid special attention to the structure of Beneventan script in its golden age, to its place in the history of medieval bookhands, and to some of the texts preserved in the script.

Fellows
Robert J. Alexander (English, Point Park College)
Betty Branch (Classics, Louisiana State University)
Clyde W. Brockett, Jr. (Choirmaster, St. Paul's, Norfolk, Virginia)
John B. Friedman (English, University of Illinois, Urbana)
Meredith P. Lillich (Fine Arts, Syracuse University)
Robert C. Rice (English, University of Oregon)

II. ARTHURIAN ROMANCE AND POLITICS

Senior Fellow: Dr. Petrus W. Tax, Professor of German, The University of North Carolina at Chapel Hill. Lecturer and Associate Professor, Johns Hopkins University (1962–68). Author, *Wort, Sinnbild, Zahl im Tristanroman: Studien zum Denken und Werten Gottfrieds von Strassburg* (1961; 2nd ed., revised and enlarged, 1971); *Notker latinus: Die Quellen zu den Psalmen, Psalm 1–50* (1972), *Psalm 51–100* (1973); "Studien zum Symbolischen in Hartmanns *Erec*: Enites Pferd," *Zeitschrift für deutsche Philologie* 82 (1963): 29–44;

"Studien zum Symbolischen in Hartmanns *Erec*: Erecs ritterliche Erhöhung," *Wirkendes Wort* 13 (1963): 277–88; *"Felix culpa* und *lapsit exillis:* Wolframs *Parzival* und die Liturgie," *Modern Language Notes* 80 (1965): 454–69; "Der *Erek* Hartmanns von Aue: Ein Antitypus zu der *Eneit* Heinrichs von Veldeke?" in *Helen Adolf Festschrift* (New York, 1968), pp. 47–62; "Wolfram von Eschenbach's *Parzival* in the Light of Biblical Typology," *Seminar* 9 (1973): 1–14; "Gahmuret zwischen Aeneas und Parzival. Zur Struktur der Vorgeschichte von Wolframs *Parzival,*" *Zeitschrift für deutsche Philologie* 92 (1973): 24–37; "Trevrizent. Die Verhüllungstechnik des Erzahlers," in *Festschrift für Hugo Moser* (Berlin, 1974), pp. 119–34; etc.

Description: Concentrating on medieval German romances and on relevant source material, the seminar explored somewhat neglected aspects of Arthurian works written in medieval Germany, such as: the romance as *Fürstenspiegel* and as a reflection of contemporary political thinking and ideology; the relationship of *Minne* and marrlage with courtly politics and power; the use of narrative structures and techniques for the creation in poetry of political conflicts and their solutions.

Fellows
William C. Crossgrove (German, Brown University)
Mary A. Grellner (English, Rhode Island College)
Thomas L. Markey (German and Linguistics, University of Michigan)
Harvey L. Sharrer (Spanish and Portuguese, University of California, Santa Barbara)

III. MEDIEVAL TRAGEDY AND NOTIONS OF TRAGEDY

Senior Fellow: Dr. Morton W. Bloomfield, Arthur Kingsley Porter Professor of English, Harvard University. Professor, The Ohio State University (1954–61). Guggenheim Fellow (1949–50; 1964–65); ACLS Fellow (1964); Fellow, Center for Advanced Study in Behavioral Sciences, Stanford, California (1967–68); Fellow, Mediaeval Academy of America, and recipient of the Haskins Medal (1964); Vice-President, American Academy of Arts and Sciences (1972–); Chairman, Planning Committee for Establishing a National Humanities Center. Author, *The Seven Deadly Sins* (East Lansing, 1952); *Piers Plowman as a Fourteenth-Century Apocalypse* (New Brunswick, N.J., 1962); *A Linguistic Introduction to the History of English*, with Leonard Newmark (New York, 1963); *Essays and Explorations* (Cambridge, Mass., 1970); *"The Man of Law's Tale*: A Tragedy of Victimization and a Christian Comedy," *Publications of the Modern Language Association* 87 (1972): 384–90; etc.

Description: The problem of medieval and Renaissance notions of tragedy both in the rhetorical and in the literary traditions. The seminar tried to classify some of the conflicting concepts of tragedy in this period. Consideration was given to medieval romances, Chaucer, Henryson, the morality play, and similar works.

Fellows
Samuel T. Cowling (English, Lake Erie College)
Georgia R. Crampton (English, Portland State University)

Appendix

Edwin D. Craun (English, Washington and Lee University)
Robert R. Edwards (English, SUNY, Buffalo)
Maureen P. A. H. Fries (English, SUNY, Fredonia)
David G. Hale (English, SUNY, Brockport)
Philip B. Rollinson (English, University of South Carolina)
Richard M. Trask (English, Frostburg State College)

IV. THE ANALYTIC ATTITUDE IN FOURTEENTH-CENTURY THOUGHT

Senior Fellow: Dr. John E. Murdoch, Professor of History of Science, Harvard University. History of Science Society, Council member (1963–69), National Science Foundation, member of Advisory Panel on History and Philosophy of Science (1964–67). Membre effectif de l'Académie Internationale d'Histoire des Sciences (1967–). Union Internationale d'Histoire et de Philosophie des Sciences, Commission pour la Collaboration d'Histoire et de Philosophie des Sciences, président (1971–). Société Internationale pour l'Étude de la Philosophie Médiévale, Assesseur (1972–). American Academy of Arts and Sciences, Fellow (1973–). Author, *Rationes mathematice. Un aspect du rapport des mathématiques et de la philosophie au moyen âge* (Paris, 1962); "Nicole Oresme's *Quaestiones super geometriam Euclidis*," *Scripta mathematica* 37 (1964): 67–91; "Two Questions on the Continuum: Walter Chatton (?), OFM, and Adam Wodeham, OFM," *Franciscan Studies* 26 (1966): 212–88; "Euclides Graeco-Latinus: A Hitherto Unknown Medieval Latin Translation of the *Elements* Made Directly from the Greek," *Harvard Studies in Classical Philology* 71 (1966): 249–302; "The Medieval Euclid: Salient Aspects of the Translation of the *Elements* by Adelard of Bath and Campanus of Novara," *Revue de Synthèse*, III sér., Nos. 49–52 (1968): 67–94; "*Mathesis in philosophiam scholasticam introducta:* The Rise and Development of the Application of Mathematics in Fourteenth Century Philosophy and Theology," in *Arts libéraux et philosophie au moyen âge (Actes du IVe Congrès International de Philosophie Médiévale;* Montreal/Paris, 1969), pp. 215–54; "Philosophy and the Enterprise of Science in the Later Middle Ages," in *The Interaction Between Science and Philosophy,* ed. Yehuda Elkana (Atlantic Highlands, N. Y., 1974): 51–74. "From Social Into Intellectual Factors: An Aspect of the Unitary Character of Late Medieval Learning," in *Cultural Context of Medieval Learning,* ed. John E. Murdoch and Edith Sylla (Dordrecht, 1975).

Description: The rise, development, and dissemination of the fourteenth-century critical and analytical approach to problems within philosophy, theology, and science, with particular attention paid to the common appeal made to new logical and scientific conceptions and techniques. Topics examined included questions about the eternity of the world, the infinite, the definition of *scientia,* motion and change, and the *potentia absoluta* of God.

Fellows
James C. Doig (Humanities, Clayton Junior College)
James K. McDonnell (Philosophy, Washington College)
Arthur S. McGrade (Philosophy, University of Connecticut)
Frederick Purnell, Jr. (Philosophy, Queens College, CUNY)

Appendix

Paul A. Streveler (Philosophy, West Chester State College)
Edith D. Sylla (History, North Carolina State University)

V. SHAKESPEARE AND EARLY DRAMA

Senior Fellow: Dr. David Bevington, Professor of English, University of Chicago. Professor, University of Virginia (1966–67). Visiting Professor at Harvard University, New York University, University of Hawaii, Northwestern University. Guggenheim Fellow (1964–65). Council member, Renaissance Society of America; member of editorial committee, Renaissance English Text Society. Editor, *The Macro Plays* (Washington, D.C., 1972); *The Complete Works of Shakespeare*, with Hardin Craig (Glenview, Illinois, 1973). Author, *From "Mankind" to Marlowe* (Cambridge, Mass., 1962); *Tudor Drama and Politics* (Cambridge, Mass., 1968); "Shakespeare the Elizabethan Dramatist," in *A New Companion to Shakespeare Studies*, ed. K. Muir and S. Schoenbaum (London, 1971); "Shakespeare vs. Jonson on Satire," in *Shakespeare 1971*, ed. Clifford Leech and J. M. R. Margeson (Toronto, 1972); etc.

Description: Comparative studies of Shakespeare's early plays in relation to the works of his predecessors and contemporaries, for example: *The Comedy of Errors* and Palutus' *Menaechmi*, or *Titus Andronicus* and Kyd's *The Spanish Tragedy*. Such aspects as sources, the development of Elizabethan dramatic genres, and problems of staging received special attention.

Fellows
John W. Doebler (English, Arizona State University)
Nancy L. Harvey (English, University of Cincinnati)
Richard S. M. Hirsch (English, Virginia Wesleyan College)
F. Whitney Jones (English, St. Andrews College)
Frederick O. Waage (English, Douglass College)
William P. Walsh (English, Butler University)

VI. EMPIRE AS FACT AND IDEA IN EARLY MODERN EUROPE

Senior Fellow: Dr. John M. Headley, Professor of History, The University of North Carolina at Chapel Hill. Chairman, Southeastern Institute of Medieval and Renaissance Studies (1967); Guggenheim Fellow (1973–74); editor, *Medieval and Renaissance Studies*, Volume III (Chapel Hill, 1968). Editor and author, *Responsio ad Lutherum*, Yale Edition of the Complete Works of St. Thomas More, vol. V (New Haven, 1969); author, *Luther's View of Church History* (New Haven, 1963); "Thomas Murner, Thomas More, and the First Expression of More's Ecclesiology," *Studies in the Renaissance*, 14 (1967): 73–92; "Luther and the Fifth Lateran Council," *Archiv für Reformationsgeschichte* 64 (1973): 55–78; "The Continental Reformation," in *The Meaning of the Renaissance and Reformation*, ed. Richard L. DeMolen (Boston, 1974), pp. 131–211; etc.

Description: A study of empire as a viable polity in Europe during the sixteenth and early seventeenth centuries. The institutional, social, and administrative aspects of empire were considered. Particular attention was given to the contemporary understanding of empire and its transformation in the revival of imperial messianism, the humanist and scholastic critiques of empire, and the justifications for the Spanish *monarquía*.

Fellows
Marvin W. Anderson (History, Bethel Seminary)
Kathleen Gavigan (History, Cabrini College)
Andrew A. Tadie (English, Kansas Newman College)
Shirley B. Whitaker (Romance Languages, The University of North Carolina at Greensboro)
Richard C. Wittenberg (History, University of Wisconsin, Milwaukee)